Cases in OPERATIONS MANAGEMENT

Cases in OPERATIONS MANAGEMENT

Jeff E. Heyl
DePaul University

Jon L. Bushnell
University of the Virgin Islands

Linda A. Stone

ADDISON-WESLEY PUBLISHING COMPANY

Reading, Massachusetts • Menlo Park, California
New York • Don Mills, Ontario • Wokingham, England
Amsterdam • Bonn • Sydney • Singapore • Tokyo
Madrid • San Juan • Milan • Paris

Senior Sponsoring Editor: Julia Berrisford
Assistant Editor: Maureen Lawson
Freelance Production Supervisor: Laura Noorda
Copyeditor: Margaret Hill
Proofreader: Phyllis Coyne
Text and Cover Designer: Marshall Henrichs
Compositor: Sigrid and Michael Wile
Illustrator: Tech-Graphics
Manufacturing Supervisor: Roy Logan
Art Editor: Susan London-Payne

Library of Congress Cataloging-in-Publication Data

Heyl, Jeff E.
    Cases in operations management / by Jeff E. Heyl, Jon L.
Bushnell, Linda A. Stone.
        p.   cm.
    ISBN 0-201-53289-1
    1. Production management--Case studies.   I. Bushnell, Jon L.
II. Stone, Linda A.   III. Title.
TS155.H44   1994
658.5--dc20   93-38543
                                                                   CIP

1 2 3 4 5 6 7 8 9 10—MA—9796959493

Preface

The case method of teaching traces its roots back at least as far as the birth of the Socratic method. In general, a case provides a controlled environment that exposes students to a considerable amount of information about a company, its history, and its current situations. This information forms the basis for discussion, analysis, and decision making. Because the environment is controlled, the pedagogical value of the exercise is maintained. Because the information is consistent and predictable, specific objectives with respect to the presentation of decision-making techniques and analysis can be accomplished. In the less controlled setting of an actual operating firm, it is sometimes quite difficult to accomplish preplanned pedagogical objectives.

This book is designed to provide new case resources for Operations Management courses. It is a series of cases that address functional-level problems which can be studied, analyzed, and resolved using the tools and techniques typically presented in the core Operations Management curriculum. Further, these cases are rich enough to simulate the dynamic nature of real-world conditions where all the desired information might not be readily available and tradeoffs among different alternatives and decisions are a common occurrence. Finally, these cases are set in firms that are representative of the organizations in which many of today's and tomorrow's graduates will seek employment. The cases are set in modern manufacturing and service organizations and include a variety of industries and sizes. In this way, students are exposed to diverse situations, settings, and conditions that can prepare them for the future.

The cases in this book come from six different companies. For each company there are three cases dealing with common Operations Management problems. Unlike most case books, the same core problems are presented in more than one company setting. This provides a great deal of flexibility for the student and the instructor. By selecting different companies, a course can focus on service organizations, manufacturing firms, or a mix of the two and still cover the basic Operations Management material. Further, the cases are cast at different levels. Some of the cases require only moderate levels of analysis to reach effective decisions. Others will require highly advanced applications of Operations Management tools to resolve. By selecting cases by subject organization and level of difficulty, the instructor can tailor the cases to the objectives of the course.

There are also two introductory cases designed to be used at the very beginning of a course. These two cases require no quantitative analysis and effectively introduce the wide variety of Operations Management issues found in most firms.

Three of the six company settings in this book, Lower Florida Keys Health System, PDQ Printing, and Transducer Technology are real firms and the cases describe real problems and the actions of real people. The other three firms, Morris Valley Estate Winery, NorthCoast Bank, and Salt River Labs, are disguised companies, but they share with the others a foundation in the real world. Although reality is a good thing to bring into the classroom, it does not always provide the best possible vehicle for teaching a particular tool, technique, or theory. In each of these cases we have taken some liberties with the truth of the matter to improve the pedagogical value of the case. No one reading these cases should rely on the information or situations presented as being precise accounts of the conditions or actions of any of the firms. The cases are modeled after reality; they are not necessarily real. The companies in this book are not always shining examples of the "correct" approach to solving classic Operations Management problems. They are real companies facing real problems, and the way they have chosen may not always be the best, but it is theirs. We can learn from the experience.

This text may be used in a wide variety of Operations Management courses. Its primary use would be in the classic Operations Management survey course at both the undergraduate and graduate level. A selection of cases from the book could be used to supplement the main text in areas selected by the instructor. Alternately, an instructor who wished to use the case method as the primary means of instruction could use this book as the main text material for an Operations Management survey course with the detailed information supplied from other sources.

The topics covered in the cases are comprehensive enough to satisfy either of these objectives.

However, the possible uses for this text go beyond the basic survey course. A carefully planned curriculum might take advantage of some of the cases in elective courses. Several of the cases deal with basic Operations Management decisions at a fairly sophisticated level. These cases could be used in advanced courses in Operations Strategy, Planning and Control Systems, Inventory, and others.

Finally, many people contributed to the creation of this book. Each of the subject companies let us take hours of their valuable time interviewing key people and collecting reams of information. The value of their cooperation cannot be overstated. The editors and staff at Addison-Wesley provided excellent guidance and exhibited great patience and understanding as we worked through the process of writing this book. They have been terrific to work with. As every author knows, writing a book takes time away from family and friends. Ours have been tolerant and forgiving. All these people have our respect and gratitude for the help and support they have provided over the past many months.

Chicago, IL   J.E.H.
St. Croix, VI   J.L.B.
Crystal Lake, IL   L.A.S.

Contents

COMPANY 1

LOWER FLORIDA KEYS HEALTH SYSTEM

CASE 1   Lower Florida Keys Health System: Quality

Rick Pederson set the just completed report of the accrediting team down on his desk with a sigh. The hospital had been accredited for three more years and his area, Quality Assurance (QA), passed cleanly. That was very good news. Accreditation team visits are stressful at the very least. Add to that the fact that Rick had only been in this job for six months, and it made for a very difficult month. "Well," he mused, "the next big item on the agenda is the implementation of the new Joint Commission on Accreditation of Healthcare Organizations (JCAHO) standards. It will be very interesting to see what changes will have to be made next year."

Rick is the Quality Assurance Coordinator for the hospital. He was moved into this position after many years in other areas of the hospital, most recently in Emergency Services. While there he ran the Quality Assurance activities for the department. His success and visibility in that role was the vehicle to the QA Coordinator position. In this position he is responsible for chairing the QA Subcommittee. This group reviews the real and potential quality problems in the hospital at monthly meetings and coordinates corrective actions. Often this involves more than one department, and Rick must coordinate these interactions. The structure of this subcommittee is somewhat complex, and an organization chart for the hospital is included as Figure 1 to help put this in perspective. There are in fact four different subcommittees that have essentially the same members. One is, of course, the QA Subcommittee. The other three committees are the Medical Records Subcommittee, the Utilization Review Subcommittee, and the Risk Management Subcommittee. Although the charge of each subcommittee is different, there is a consid-

Figure 1   *Lower Florida Keys Health System Organizational Chart*

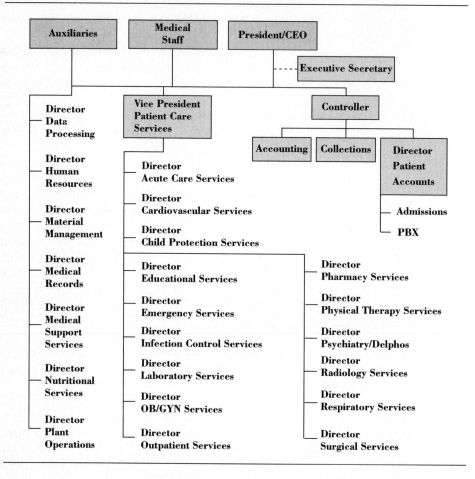

erable amount of overlap between the functions. It makes good sense for these subcommittees to be one group.

For example, the Utilization Review Subcommittee is charged with examining all patient cases to see if they meet the criteria for admission and, during their stay, to determine if the treatment being provided is appropriate given their illness or injury. This is an extremely important function since third-party payers such as Medicare or Blue Cross/Blue Shield essentially require such review to support payment claims made to them. They don't want to pay for unnecessary or inappropriate services or treatment. On the other hand, the hospital needs to ensure that patients receive all the care and treatment indicated by their conditions.

Utilization Review looks at both of these aspects of the care provided. The link with QA is fairly clear. Inappropriate or insufficient care is a potential quality problem. Because these two subcommittees comprise the same people, all real or potential problems are quite visible.

In theory, the QA Subcommittee sees all QA issues and problems and initiates appropriate actions. In practice, each department has its own QA function. It reviews and reports on its activities periodically to the QA Subcommittee. Rick prepares a summary of these reports, highlighting issues that seem important, and presents it to a committee from the medical staff. This Medical Staff Committee then distributes the information to the rest of the doctors.

Not all departments report at the same meetings, and this occasionally causes some problems. Each department reports quarterly, and only three departments typically report at any one meeting. If an interdepartmental problem comes up at the meeting and all involved departments are not present, Rick has to wait until after the meeting, schedule individual meetings with the appropriate people, and review the problem with them. This multiple-step process is usually effective, but it is sometimes cumbersome and often causes nuances to be lost. A face-to-face discussion is almost always a better way to identify and resolve problems between departments. There has been some discussion about changing this structure, but nothing has happened yet. The new JCAHO standards will require at least one change. They require that all the top administration be actively involved in the QA process. The monthly QA Committee meetings must now include the president, vice president, and all department directors.

"That will be one more of several changes we'll have to make in the next few months," Rick thought as he sat back in his chair. The new JCAHO standards are the easiest to manage. Because the life of the entire organization depends on meeting whatever standards JCAHO sets, it is a simple matter for Rick to say, "Here they are; we have to meet them." (A section of the JCAHO standards and the hospital implementation plan to meet them is included as Table 1.) Everyone in the entire organization knows the importance of meeting the standards, so there is little real resistance. That is not the same as saying everyone truly understands and agrees with the reasons for the change, but they will do what is required.

To *really* integrate QA into the fabric of the hospital, however, Rick is going to have to develop and provide some new educational programs. QA is going to be an ever-increasing part of life at the hospital. Some of the administrators and directors are very much up to speed on QA issues, but others are not. They are going along with the changes because they know it is a necessity, but they do not really understand the activity at a fundamental level.

TABLE 1 Lower Florida Keys Health System QA Plan. JCAHO
Standards Analysis

QA Plan Language	JCAHO QA Standard
Clinic privileges of physicians and allied health professionals will be reviewed as outlined in the Medical Staff By-Laws, and other hospital professional staff credentials will be reviewed on a periodic basis. Input from Quality review activities will be used to assure that privileges, privilege delineation, and credentials are commensurate with the practitioner's actual practice and abilities. Documentation of current license and current competence are a prerequisite to the medical staff privileges as well as employment in a technical or professional health care capacity.	QA.2 The scope of the quality assurance program includes at least the activities listed in Required Characteristics QA.2.1 through QA.2.5.3 and described in other chapters of the Manual. Required Characteristics QA.2.1 The following medical staff functions are performed: QA.2.1.1 The monitoring and evaluation of the quality and appropriateness of patient care and the clinical performance of all individuals with clinical privileges.
Monthly meetings of the medical staff shall consider findings from the ongoing monitoring activities of the medical staff; surgical case review, drug usage evaluation, medical record review function, blood usage review, and pharmacy and therapeutics function.	QA.2.1.1.1 Monthly meetings of clinical departments or major clinical services (or the medical staff, for nondepartmentalized medical staff) to consider findings from the ongoing monitoring activities of the medical staff. (Medical Staff Standard MS.3)
Surgical procedures will be reviewed to assure that proper documentation supports the need for surgery and that the diagnosis and surgical outcome is supported by appropriate clinical and ancillary tests. Such review includes tissue, nontissue and therapeutic procedures and pre-operative versus post-operative diagnosis and management. Monitoring and evaluation activities will be conducted monthly.	QA.2.1.1.2 Surgical cases review. (Medical Staff Standard MS.6)
Drug evaluation and utilization monitoring shall be performed to maintain usage in accordance with acceptable standards and to minimize drug reactions. Every effort will be made to reduce medication errors to the lowest acceptable level. Minimum review includes drugs known	QA.2.1.1.3 Drug usage evaluation. (Medical Staff Standard MS.6)

(continued)

TABLE 1 **(continued)**

to be high cost, have significant potential for adverse reactions or interaction and interventions and antibiotics.	
Completeness and timeliness of medical record documentation monitoring shall be performed to maintain a sufficiently detailed record which provides a pertinent account of the patient's condition, hospital course, and management. The process outcome of patient care should be adequately reflected in each record.	QA.2.1.1.4 The medical record review function. (Medical Staff Standard MS.6)

This lack of true understanding may be even more pronounced at the lower levels of the organization. Rick is quite sure that most nurses, for example, do not have a clear picture of their role in the quality process. If you were to ask them, they would say they have little or no involvement. This is not to say they are not working hard to provide high-quality care for their patients, but they view it as an individual effort, not as part of the big process. All they really see of the process is the feedback they get on their performance review. Even then, the linkage between their actions and the numbers the QA system reports is not made clear to them. Rick raised his eyebrows as he thought about the whole topic of performance review. "What a great place to send the important messages about quality, but it is really not being done. This will probably require a complete redesign of the review system. Well," he grinned, "that would certainly get everyone's attention!"

The general lack of understanding is going to have to change. Rick knows that unless there is complete commitment and understanding from the top of the organization all the way to very bottom, QA will never become fully integrated into the organization. Fortunately this process will be made somewhat easier because JCAHO is continually requiring greater and greater involvement by all levels of administrators and staff.

"Maybe a new approach to the education program will help," Rick mused. "So far, all the different education sessions I have put together have targeted very specific needs and were really useful to only a small group of people." For example, last year Rick went around to most of the departments teaching them how to comply with the JCAHO ten-step monitoring and evaluation process for QA activities. This required developing department-specific goals and standards, so only parts of the core material were common to all training sessions. However, the new JCAHO guidelines mandate a broader form of education concentrating on the concepts of quality improvement, not just a specific quality assurance tool. Further, this education must include the highest levels of the organization.

Perhaps more importantly, education has a role that Rick has not yet been able to address at all—education's role in corrective action. A few months ago a problem was resolved through education targeted at corrective action. One of the doctors was using an older surgical procedure for a particular condition. Although this older procedure was safe, there was a newer, preferred procedure that was much faster and required a far shorter recuperation period. As a result, this doctor's name would show up every once in a while in Utilization Review meetings. The QA Subcommittee picked up on this, as did the medical staff. The problem was simple to resolve. This particular doctor had never been trained on the newer technique and was, correctly, reluctant to experiment. Two other doctors in the hospital worked with him to provide the training he needed and the problem has been resolved.

Although in this situation Rick could not actually provide the necessary training, the idea is important for the organization. It has applications in every area of the hospital, and in some of these situations, Rick *can* provide the necessary educational programs. "Of course, more education is going to require more staff time." The thought brought a painful smile to Rick's face. The hospital, like many organizations, very carefully watches the number of full-time equivalent (FTE) employees. This is its measure of staffing levels. "That may be the hardest battle. When push comes to shove on the budget battle lines, immediate patient care must come before training classes."

The FTE problem is significant. Many people in the hospital see it as a nearly insurmountable obstacle. At last month's QA Subcommittee meeting there was a great example of this situation. Two departments were pointing fingers at each other, each blaming the other for incomplete charts and slow work. They each claimed they had no extra time, no extra FTEs, to do the other department's work. And they were right, as far as they went. Resources are scarce at the hospital, and no one can afford to be doing another's work. The real difficulty, however, was not with the scarce resources or with incomplete charts. The hurdle was the focus on FTEs, not the actual process. They were shocked to see how quickly the problem was resolved, Rick remembered, when he suggested they stop looking at the amount of time it was taking to handle this problem and try to fix the process instead. They made a few small changes to the chart maintenance and distribution process that required no additional work and the problem hasn't occurred since.

A recent problem in Respiratory Services is another example of the hurdle the FTE-based outlook presents. One of the respiratory technicians' tasks had been to verify the settings of the respiratory equipment for each patient. They would compare the doctor's orders to the actual settings and record their verification on the patient chart. The technicians often complained that this was a frustrating and time-consuming task. The time they spent on it interfered with their ability to do more meaningful work. The attitude was "fit it in the day somehow; we have all this work to do." The focus was just on the time the job took. Rick suggested that they fully investigate the processes involved to see if any changes could be made. It turned out that there was no need for this job at all. The floor nurses were setting and checking the equipment, and they were doing it accurately. This particular task was eliminated, and the technicians could now spend more time working directly with patients with more difficult and challenging problems.

Another problem facing Rick is the nature of the actual QA measures developed and used in the hospital. Currently two separate sets of measures are being collected. The first is a patient questionnaire administered to all patients at discharge. (The results of a recent six-month period are reported in Table 2.) Since this form is voluntary, not all patients complete it.

The second set of measures is derived from the quarterly report each department makes to the QA Subcommittee. A typical report presents the acceptable and unacceptable activities in a department during a quarter. The actual form varies somewhat from department to department, limiting the degree to which the information can be compared. Each department has a QA Plan, and these plans all specify the important dimensions of patient care for that individual department. Table 3 contains excerpts from the QA Plan for Surgical Services, and Table 4 summarizes Surgical Services reports for the same six months. Table 5 is an example of the Monitoring and Evaluation Tracking Log for Surgical Services for the latter part of 1991 and the first quarter of 1992.

Rick would like to be able to compare the results of the two different systems, patient surveys and department reports, to see if they reveal any differences. This is not easily done. Not only do they cover different aspects of patient care and report them in different forms, but there are some questions about the reliability of patient-developed measures. It

TABLE 2   Lower Florida Keys Health System Patient Questionnaire Summary

Questions	\multicolumn{12}{c}{Percentage Yes/No Responses}

Questions	May Y	May N	Jun Y	Jun N	Jul Y	Jul N	Aug Y	Aug N	Sep Y	Sep N	Oct Y	Oct N
Prompt registration	90	4	94	0	93	1	94	0	88	6	88	6
Courteous registration	89	1	90	0	90	0	90	0	90	0	89	1
Uncomplicated registration	83	10	82	11	89	4	78	15	77	16	81	12
Satisfactory insurance/financing	94	2	96	0	95	1	94	2	92	4	93	3
Satisfactory planning for release	96	0	95	1	96	0	95	1	96	0	95	1
Explanation of care/tests/treatments	98	2	98	2	99	1	98	2	98	2	98	2
Staff identify themselves	98	1	99	0	98	1	99	0	98	1	98	1
Nurses prompt	90	4	92	2	92	2	91	3	92	2	93	1
Nurses caring	96	1	97	0	96	1	96	1	97	0	97	0
Nurses respectful of privacy	93	1	93	1	93	1	94	0	94	0	94	0
Satisfactory care by radiology	72	1	72	1	72	1	72	1	72	1	73	0
Satisfactory care by laboratory	71	0	70	1	71	0	70	1	70	1	71	0
Satisfactory care by respiratory therapy	38	1	38	1	38	1	38	1	38	1	38	1
Satisfactory care by physical therapy	33	1	33	1	34	0	33	1	34	0	33	1
Satisfactory care by surgery	54	2	56	0	55	1	56	0	54	2	56	0
Satisfactory care by volunteers	61	1	62	0	61	1	62	0	62	0	61	1
Satisfactory care by telephone operator	70	4	73	1	70	4	71	3	71	3	70	4
Room clean	98	1	99	0	97	2	99	0	99	0	99	0
Room quiet	91	1	89	3	91	1	87	5	88	4	87	5
Room comfortable	92	1	91	2	92	1	91	2	92	1	90	3
Food appetizing	81	16	84	13	90	7	78	19	84	13	84	13
Food served in timely manner	95	2	96	1	97	0	95	2	97	0	97	0
Total Patients Surveyed	52		50		61		58		55		75	

Note: Totals may not equal 100% due to nonresponses by patients or service not provided.

TABLE 3   Department of Surgery Surgical and Anesthesia Services Quality Assurance Plan

Overview

The goal of the Surgical Department Quality Assurance Program is to systematically and continuously monitor and evaluate the quality and appropriateness of surgical- and anesthesia-related care provided to the Lower Florida Keys Health System. A ten-step program to monitor and evaluate patient care quality has been developed and is described herein. The collection of departmental statistics and a mechanism of daily chart review have been incorporated into this plan.

Ten Step Monitoring and Evaluation Process

Step 1:   Responsibility
Responsibilities are as defined in the following chart:

	QA Committee	Chief of Surgery	Dir. Surgery and Amb. Care	Supervisor, Surgery	Nursing Staff
1. Overall responsibility	X	X			
2. Scope of care	X	X	X		
3. Aspects of care		X	X	X	X
4. Indicators		X	X	X	X
5. Thresholds		X	X	X	
6. Collect data		X	X	X	X
7. Evaluate care		X	X	X	
8. Take action	X	X	X		
9. Assess actions		X	X	X	
10. Report information		X	X	X	

(continued)

TABLE 3 (continued)

Step 2: Scope of Care

Patients of all ages ranging from pediatrics to geriatrics. Patients of all medical conditions ranging from normal, healthy individuals to critically ill. Services include but are not limited to surgical treatment of the following conditions and diagnoses:

Condition	Service
General surgery	Full
Orthopedics	Full
Obstetrics and Gynecology	Full
Urology	Full
Cardio-Thoracic	Limited
Pediatrics	Limited
Ophthalmology	Limited

Treatment, care, and services are provided by the following categories of personnel:

Physicians and Surgeons   Nurse Practitioners
Dentists   Registered Nurses
CRNAs   OR Technicians
Physician Assistants   Anesthesia Technicians

This department looks to the following agencies and organizations for guidelines and references when developing departmental standards of care:

State and federal governmental agencies

JCAHO
AORN
ASPAN
Physicians' professional organizations

Step 3: Important Aspects of Care

The routine collection of data relevant to quality assurance in the Department of Surgery may be performed either prospectively or retrospectively. The aspects of care chosen for review will reflect areas of high patient risk and/or areas of nursing concern. These parameters will be reviewed annually to ensure appropriateness and are subject to addition, deletion, or revision as deemed necessary. The following items are the aspects of care currently under study:

Pre-Operative Indicators

	Thresholds (%)
1. Correct patient transported to OR/RR	100
2. Consent correct/complete/signed	100
3. History and physical dictated and/or on chart	95
4. Pre-OP orders completed	95
5. Pre-OP vital signs documented	95
6. Allergies noted	100
7. Patient ID band on patient	95

Intra-Operative Indicators

	Thresholds (%)
8. Break in sterile technique	0
9. Incorrect sponge/needle/instrument count	5
10. Incorrect anesthetic agent administered	0
11. Tracheal reevaluation necessary	5
12. Intra-operative death	0
13. Respiratory arrest in non-intubated patients	5
14. Intra-operative myocardial infarction	0
15. Dental injury during anesthesia	0
16. Unplanned admission to ICU post-anesthesia	0
17. Unplanned disconnection of life support equipment	0
18. Lack of timely intervention/vital sign abnormality	0

(continued)

13

TABLE 3 (continued)

Intra-Operative Indicators	Thresholds (%)
19. Incorrect patient anesthetized/surgerized	0
20. Incorrect procedure/procedure not on consent	0
21. Unplanned removal/repair of organ/body part	0

Post-Operative Indicators	Thresholds (%)
22. Post-anesthesia care greater than two hours	10
23. Death in post-anesthesia area	0
24. Acute myocardial infarction in PACU	0
25. Neurological deficit not present pre-operatively	0
26. Re-intubation necessary post-OP	5
27. Adult patients with pulse <40 or >120	2
28. Adult patients with temperature <96 or >101	2
29. Adult patients with BP <70 or >200 systolic	2

Step 4: Indicators

An indicator is a quality-related variable that can be easily and reliably measured, for example, Correct Intervention, Complication, Outcome, or Staff Error. Indicators will be selected and developed as necessary.

Step 5: Thresholds

Reporting thresholds will be determined to indicate at what level an evaluation becomes necessary. Each indicator will be assigned a separate threshold.

Step 6: Collection and Organization of Data

For each indicator, staff will collect performance data on an ongoing basis. QA data may be collected from Patient Records, Incident Reports, Direct Observation, or Surveys. The staff of the Surgical Department will collect this data under the supervision of the Chief, Director, and Supervisor of Surgery. Data collection will be accomplished by the use of appropriate forms and will not fall below a 10% frequency threshold.

Step 7: Evaluation

When the data reach the threshold for evaluation, assigned staff members shall evaluate the care provided to determine whether a problem or opportunity to improve care is present. The care provided by physicians and other credentialed providers shall be evaluated by the Chief of Surgery. The OR Director and Supervisor will evaluate the nonphysician components of care.

Step 8: Corrective Actions

It is the responsibility of the Chief of Surgery (or his or her designee) to recommend to the QA Committee any corrective action that may be necessary for those problems found during the evaluation of care. It will be the responsibility of the QA Committee to accept or modify these recommendations and to determine the nature and timing of any corrective action that may be necessary.

Step 9: Action Assessment

The results of continued monitoring and evaluation activities shall be documented to provide a record of efficacy of corrective actions taken. If no improvement is noted, reevaluation shall be performed and a new corrective action taken.

Step 10: Reporting

The Chief, Director, and Supervisor of Surgery shall submit a report to the QA Committee on a quarterly basis.

TABLE 4   Operating Room QA Report May 1992 – October 1992

	Number of Dropouts					
Indicator	M	J	J	A	S	O
1	0	0	0	0	0	0
2	0	0	0	0	0	0
3	0	0	0	0	0	0
4	2	0	1	3	0	5
5	1	1	1	0	1	4
6	1	0	0	1	0	3
7	2	3	3	1	0	4
8	18	20	20	19	17	27
9	18	20	21	19	17	28
10	18	20	21	19	17	28
11	18	20	21	19	17	28
12	18	20	21	19	17	28
13	18	20	21	19	17	28
14	18	20	21	19	17	28
15	18	20	21	19	17	28
16	18	20	21	19	17	28
17	18	20	21	19	17	28
18	18	20	21	19	17	28
19	18	20	21	19	17	28
20	18	20	21	19	17	28
21	18	20	21	19	17	28
22	18	20	21	19	17	28
23	18	20	21	19	17	28
24	18	20	21	19	17	28
25	18	20	21	19	17	28
26	18	20	21	19	17	28
27	18	19	20	19	17	26
28	18	20	21	19	17	28
29	17	18	20	19	17	25
Total Patients	18	20	21	19	17	28

TABLE 5 Monitoring and Evaluation Tracking Log. 1st Quarter 1992

Surgery and anesthesia services   *Responsible individual: Chief & Director of Surgery*

Problem Description	Date Identified	Problem Analysis	Corrective Action	Follow-Up Action	Results of Action
Pre-OP orders not completed (Indicator 4)	This quarter	Floor nurses missing pre-OP orders, esp. on-call antibiotics and anxiolytics	Problem brought to attention of Dept. Director		Observe next quarter stats
Pre-OP vital signs not done/charted (Indicator 5)	This quarter	Failure of floor nurse to take/chart pre-OP vitals	See above		See above
Allergies not noted on chart (Indicator 6)	This quarter	Allergies noted on pre-OP interview, not written on front of chart	See above		See above
Break in sterile technique (Indicator 7)	This quarter	Nurses and resp. therapy techs frequently contaminate the sterile Kreissleman	Will offer in-service classes on OR technique		See above
Incorrect needle count (Indicator 8)	11/20/91	Surgeon dropped needle on floor; X-ray of patient negative	None		See above

(continued)

TABLE 5 (continued) Follow-up Report 1991

Surgery and anesthesia services   *Responsible individual: Chief & Director of Surgery*

Problem Description	Date Identified	Problem Analysis	Corrective Action	Follow-Up Action	Results of Action
Consents not signed (Indicator 2)	1991	Consents not signed on floor or in pre-OP	Communication with floor staff, supervisors, and director was successful in decreasing # of omissions	None	No errors this quarter
H&P not dictated (Indicator 3)	1991	Unable to ascertain if H&P had been dictated	Physicians asked to state status of H&P prior to surgery	None	No errors this quarter
BP (Indicator 2)	1991	BP limits set too strictly	Reset limits to realistic parameters	None	No dropouts & no patients requiring treatment under old guidelines

would be very nice if the two different systems reported something like the same information. This would certainly simplify the comparison of the two sets of results. However, this might not be at all feasible. Each department needs to monitor and report dimensions specific to its work, and patients have a very different view of quality of care than does the hospital. It might seem cynical, but there are patients who will rate the quality of their care very high merely because they got a back rub every night and the food was fine. Although these factors are important, the department might be far more interested in the timeliness and accuracy of medication, a complete medical history including allergies, and proper measurement of vital signs. Still, the viewpoint of the patients is important because they are customers. Effort to improve the systems needs to be made despite the problems.

Emergency Services and Surgical Services are trying a new approach. They have developed and are attempting to implement concurrent review procedures. The idea is to collect and report information about patient care while it is actually happening. Right now the information gets collected and reported as much as three months later. However, concurrent review places an extra burden on every care provider in the hospital. They can no longer wait until a slow period, perhaps hours later, to complete the necessary paperwork. It has to be done as it is happening. The two departments are doing a pretty good job, but some things are still falling through the cracks of the concurrent process. They ultimately get picked up in the retrospective review, but immediacy is lost.

A situation that complicates this effort is the limited capability of the hospital's information system. The QA function clearly could benefit from a more detailed analysis of the information they routinely collect. For example, a case might come to the Risk Management Committee concerning a patient fall. Each such case is fully investigated, but they are all treated individually. If the underlying problem is the technique of one particular nurse, this would only show up in an analysis of many such incidents over time. But it is difficult to enter this type of data in the system and even more difficult to analyze data once it's there. Further, some departments have discrete systems that work for them but don't communicate with other areas of the hospital. The quarterly Department QA reports are a good example. Even if a department prepares the report on a computer, Rick has to reenter the results in his system in order to prepare summary reports. "Things are changing pretty fast around here," Rick thought. "Maybe this is the time to develop a request for a real information system that could facilitate the QA process. I guess that will go on the 'To Do' list as well."

CASE 2   Lower Florida Keys Health System: Forecasting, Capacity, Scheduling, and Queuing

"You just never know what is going to come in the door," thought Gayle. "I guess having that dental surgery suite really is a good idea, even if we do joke about it being a 'once a year' room."

Gayle Gordon is the Department Director for Emergency Services at the Lower Florida Keys Health System (LFKHS) hospital in Key West, Florida. She had been called in at 2:00 AM this morning for an unusual case, even by Emergency Room (ER) standards. A young woman had accidentally shot herself in the jaw, mistaking a loaded revolver for an asthma inhaler in her sleep. She was very fortunate. Her jaw was slightly damaged and a tooth was destroyed, but not much else. It was no problem for the ER staff to stabilize the patient and control the basic trauma. The reason Gayle was called was the oral surgery suite. It was needed for the first time in many months.

Many years ago the hospital had installed a dedicated oral surgery suite. It was used so infrequently that the hospital staff joked about it being a "once a year" room. In fact, during much of the year it served as an unofficial warehouse and conference room. The suite wasn't very large, about 90 square feet, and was in a corner of the general operating room area (see Figure 1). It might seem like a conspicuous waste, but a hospital in Key West has to deal with unusual circumstances. The Lower Florida Keys Health System hospital is the only one in Key West and the only major hospital south of Miami. It's about 130 miles to Miami, and that's too far for some things. The oral surgery suite is just one example of the type of commitment the hospital has to make because of its rather rural location. The patient tonight required oral surgery. It was no prob-

Figure 1 *Floor Plan of LFKHS First Floor*

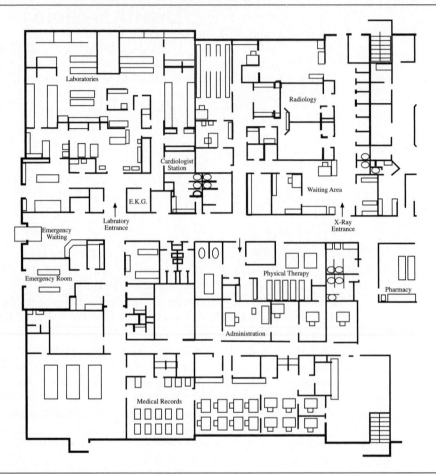

lem getting the doctor and staff together to actually perform the surgery, but they had to clean out the room first! "Well," thought Gayle, "that must be part of the boss's job! It's time to be here anyway. I might as well start on the schedules for next month."

Since Gayle became the Department Director for Emergency Service, she had been collecting detailed records on the amount of traffic in the Emergency Room (ER). Not surprisingly, it varied considerably. The most recent data she has is for March, April, and May. The June data is incomplete, but two months should be enough to develop a forecast for

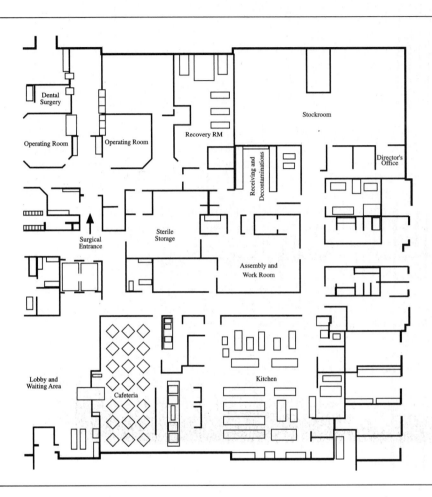

July. She has been working in Key West for six years and has a good perspective on the demand for ER services. For example, she knows from experience that the summer months are about 20% slower than the winter and feels that the demand during March was about right for the normal winter months. The summer lull, if that's what you can call it, starts right after the Spring Break rush. Further, the population in the Lower Keys seems to have stabilized in the last few years at about 30,000 people. The area has seen very little growth, and the projections are for this to continue in the foreseeable future. Gayle needs to make sure she has enough nurses scheduled to cover the expected demand. Table 1 shows the number of new patients in ER each hour for March, April, and May of this year. ER is typically staffed by one doctor during the summer months and two in the winter. This assignment is made by the Medical Director and isn't part of Gayle's scheduling activities.

Gayle has been successful in implementing one of her most important projects in ER at LFKHS. She has made sure that all the nurses who staff the facility have the same basic set of skills. This has required some considerable effort. Although there are some differences in actual experience, all 16 nurses in ER are RNs and all have taken the Basic Critical Care and Advanced Cardiac Life Support courses. Most have completed the Trauma Nursing Core Curriculum and all will within their first year of employment. Additionally, almost all the nurses have passed the Certified Emergency Nursing Test. This uniformly high level of training allows Gayle to treat the nurses as essentially interchangeable. It makes her life much easier.

She still has some problems, though. Each shift requires a designated Triage nurse. All patients entering ER are classified in one of four different acuity categories, 1 through 4. Patients in categories 1 and 2 are sent directly to an examining room because they are the most serious. Category 3 and 4 patients are seen by the Triage nurse for basic first aid and decisions related to tests, X-rays, and so forth. Fast Track patients are also identified at this point. The Fast Track system was introduced shortly after the first of the year to identify those patients who really shouldn't be in ER at all. Their condition is not really that serious, and they should be going to a clinic or their private doctor. The goal is to get the Fast Track people out in under one hour. Understandably the Triage nurse post requires considerable experience and the ability to make correct decisions quickly. Gayle has only five nurses she feels she can put in this post at this time.

Gayle knows from experience that the nurses can comfortably and safely work 12-hour shifts. She needs to have 24-hour coverage by Triage nurses. Overtime is paid on anything over 12 hours a day or 40 hours a week. It is possible to schedule overtime, but Gayle is constantly trying to reduce this. Scheduled overtime is way down this year, about 60% of last year's figures, and this is good news. Even when overtime is scheduled, it is often not worked. If things are slow, the people on overtime are sent home. Likewise, if the demand is greater than expected, nurses from the next shift can be called in early. Gayle also considers the personal wishes of the nurses as best she can in these schedules. For example, she has one nurse who likes to be scheduled 12 hours per day for six days in a row. She then gets three days off. One of her nurses can

TABLE 1 Emergency Room Patient Arrivals. March 1992

Time \ Date	S 1	M 2	T 3	W 4	T 5	F 6	S 7	S 8	M 9	T 10	W 11	T 12	F 13	S 14	S 15	M 16	T 17	W 18	T 19	F 20	S 21	S 22	M 23	T 24	W 25	T 26	F 27	S 28	S 29	M 30	T 31	Total
2400–0100		1				1	2	1	2	2	1	3	3	1	2	2	5	1	1	2	3	2	3	4	3	1	3	1	3	3	2	55
0100–0200	1	2			1		1	3	1		2			1	1	2	1			1	2	1	2	2	1	1	2	1	1	4	2	33
0200–0300	4	1	1	1		2	2	3			1				2	1	1				1	1	2	2	3	3	2	1	2	1		30
0300–0400	3	2	1	1		1		1		2	1	2		1	4	1		1			2	2	2	3	1	1		2	4	1		35
0400–0500				1							1		3	1	1				1		2			1				3		1		16
0500–0600		1							2	1						2								1	1	1	2			2	1	16
0600–0700	2	2	3	1					2	2	1	1	1		1	1	1	1	1	5		1	2	1		1		1	2		2	34
0700–0800	1	1	1	1	1	1	3	2	1	1	1			1			3	3	1	3	3		1	1	3	3	4	1	3	1	1	42
0800–0900	1	4	2	3	2	2	4	1	2	4	2	7	2	3	3	2	5	4	2	6	4	1	2	2	5	4	4	1	2	1	1	86
0900–1000	2	2	6	3	4	8	2	6	5	4	5	3	6	3	7	5	9	5	3	3	6	5	5	3	4	4	2	3	2	4	2	130
1000–1100	9	6	3	3	4	2	8	4	7	4	3	4	8	2	3	4	5	4	1	3	5	5	2	5	3	5	7	2	5	6	4	133
1100–1200	4	5	7	3	2	3	3	4	3	6	2	2	3	7	6	2	2	3	5	5	4	4	2	5	4	1	5	4	6	2	3	116
1200–1300	2	3	4	3	2	3	1	4	4	4	4	2	2	5	6	1	5	3	2	4	4	3	2	5	4	2	2	1	3	2	3	93
1300–1400	5	6		1		2	6	5	4	4	5	3	2	3	3	2	3	4	2	2	3	8	2	3	3	2	2	5	4	1	3	113
1400–1500	1	1	6	7	4	3	1	7	2	1	2	3	2	7	2	7	7	2	6	5	3	9	4	1	7	2	2	5	5	4	8	129
1500–1600	3	7	3	5	2	1	5	3	3	2	3	4	3	3	5	4	4	2	1	3	3	6	7	5	6	3	2	4	4	2	2	110
1600–1700	1	5	2	2	6	7	5	3	1	3	2	2	2	6	6	4		3	7	2	3	2	4	3	5	1	2	3	3	3	2	102
1700–1800	3	4	6	6	3	5	1	6	1	4	3	3	4	2	2	2	1	3	7	2	2	4	7	2	4	3	1	4	3	3	3	108
1800–1900	3	1	2	3	1	1	5	5	2	5	5	5	5	2	2	3	3	2	4	4	4	3	7	1	2	2	5	5	6	3		92
1900–2000	4	4	4	4	2	3		3	1	4	4	1	6	1	1	2	3	2	2	2	1	1	3	2	2	3	3	2	2	3	2	83
2000–2100	6	3	3	2	5		2	5	5	5	1	3	5	3	3	3	4	4	2	3	3	2	2	3	3	1	3	3	1	3	4	84
2100–2200	2	2	2	3		3	4		5	1	2	2	1	1	5	2	1	1	3	3	3	3	3	1	3	2	1	2	4	2	2	66
2200–2300	2	1	2	2	1	3	4		2	4	4	4	4	4	3	3	3	4	3	2	3	3	5			3	4	5	3	2	4	81
2300–2400	2	1	1	1	2		1	3	2	1		2	2	3	2	1	2	1	1	1	3	2	1	3	1	1		3	1	4	2	49
Total	59	59	55	47	52	63	68	59	62	49	53	59	65	72	55	66	51	47	65	67	69	64	46	67	48	62	65	75	51	57	
	S	M	T	W	T	F	S	S	M	T	W	T	F	S	S	M	T	W	T	F	S	S	M	T	W	T	F	S	S	M	T	

(continued)

TABLE 1 (continued) April 1992

Time	Date	1 W	2 T	3 F	4 S	5 S	6 M	7 T	8 W	9 T	10 F	11 S	12 S	13 M	14 T	15 W	16 T	17 F	18 S	19 S	20 M	21 T	22 W	23 T	24 F	25 S	26 S	27 M	28 T	29 W	30 T	Total
2400–0100		2	1	2		2			3	6	1	1	1				2	2	1			4		3	1	1	3	1	2	1	1	42
0100–0200		2		3			2		2	1	1	3		1	4	2	1	1	1		2		1	1	1	2	2	2	2	1	1	36
0200–0300				1	1	1	1	3	1	1	2	2	1			2	1		1	1	1	1			1	1	2	2	2			23
0300–0400			1		1	1				1	3		2			1	1	1	1	1	1	1		2	2		2			2	1	24
0400–0500		1	1		2			2	1		2				1	1	1			1	1	1			1				3			16
0500–0600				3	3	1	1	1		2		2	1	1					2	2	2	1		2	1	2						17
0600–0700		1			2	1	2	2	2	2	1	1	1		1	1	1	1	1	1	1			2	1	2	1	1	1		1	25
0700–0800		5	1	2	3	3	2	2	2	3	4	1	2	2	3	3	3	1	4	4	1	1	2	2	1	1	1	2		2	3	44
0800–0900		1	5	3	2	3	3	2	3	1	2	3	3	3	1	3	2	1	1	3	3	3	3	5	2	1	4	3	2	6	5	78
0900–1000		3	4	4	3	5	2	3	3	2	3	5	5	3	3	4	4	4	4	4	4	2	2	3	2	2	5	1	2	3	5	91
1000–1100		2	2	5	3	1	3	4	3	4	6	6	3	6	4	4	4	3	3	4	4	4	2	4	3	4	4	3	2	6	2	96
1100–1200		5	3	4	2	1	2	1	5	2	3	3	2	4	2	5	2	5	5	5	5	5	4	1	1	1	1	3	3	4	3	77
1200–1300		1	1	1	4	2	1	2	4	2	3	2	4	5		3	4	1	1	3	5	4	1	3	1	1	3	2	3	4	4	79
1300–1400		7	4	5	5	3	4	1	1	2	2	2	5	2		3	1	1	2	4	1	4	4		2	1	3	6	2	2	7	79
1400–1500		3	2	2	4	3	3	3	5	1	2	3	1	1	3	3	3	3	2	4	1	3	3	2	3	2	5	6	3	2	3	84
1500–1600		2	3		5	3	3	3	1	4	2	5	5	5	1	1	4	1	1	3	2	5	5	3	4	4	3	2	5	3	4	86
1600–1700		2	5	3	4	4	5	1	3	3	3	3	2	3	4	2	2	2	5	5	2	2	1	1	3	6	3	2	2	3	4	84
1700–1800		5	3	3	5	1	2	4	4	3	3	1	3	5	5	3	3		2	3	3	5	5	5	5	6	4	2	1	3	4	86
1800–1900		6	1	2	3	2	3	3	2	2	3	2	6	3			1	2	4	4			1	6	1	2	5	4	3	6	5	86
1900–2000		1	5	1	2	7	2	5	1	2	4	6	3	3	5	2	2	3	1	1	2	1	3	6	5	2	2	1	1	2	5	66
2000–2100		3	2	2	1	7	2	2		2	4	4	4	4	5	2	6	4	3	4	4	7	2	3	5	2	2	4	1	3	4	86
2100–2200		1	2	3	6	3	5	5	2	5	2	3	3	2	3	3	2	3	4	1	1	4	1	2	1	3	3	1	3	5	2	87
2200–2300		3	1	1	2	3	3	5	1	2	1	2	2	1	6	6	3	4	1	4	2	2	2	3	5	5	4	1	1	3	4	75
2300–2400		1	2	2	1	1	1	3		1	3	1	1		1	1	1	1	4	4	2	2	1	1	2	1	4	4	1	1	1	39
Total		56	44	42	65	59	44	53	46	48	41	59	61	46	31	54	49	38	38	54	41	51	41	48	51	51	71	50	46	60	68	
		W	T	F	S	S	M	T	W	T	F	S	S	M	T	W	T	F	S	S	M	T	W	T	F	S	S	M	T	W	T	

(continued)

TABLE 1 (continued) May 1992

Time	F 1	S 2	S 3	M 4	T 5	W 6	T 7	F 8	S 9	S 10	M 11	T 12	W 13	T 14	F 15	S 16	S 17	M 18	T 19	W 20	T 21	F 22	S 23	S 24	M 25	T 26	W 27	T 28	F 29	S 30	S 31	Total
2400–0100	2				1		1	1	1	2		2		3	2	1	2		5		1	2	2	1	2	2	2		3	1	2	41
0100–0200	3	1		2	2	1	1		2	3	1			1		1	1	2	1		1	1	3	1	3	2	1	1	2	1	1	38
0200–0300	1		3		1	1	1		2	2							2	1	1					1	2	1	1	1	2	2	2	24
0300–0400			2	1	1			1		1		2	1	2		1	3	1	1				2	2	2	3	1	1		2	3	32
0400–0500		1	3	2	1	1							1			3	1	1			1		2	1			1	1		3		16
0500–0600	2	1						3			2	1							2								1	1	2			16
0600–0700	1		2	1	2	1			3		2	1	1		1		1	1	1		1	4		1	1	1	1	1	1	1	2	30
0700–0800			1	1		1	1	1	3	2	1	1	1	1		1				3	1	3	3	1	1	1	1	3	4	3	3	42
0800–0900	1	1	1	4	2	3	2	2	4	1	2	4	2	6	2	3	3	2	4	4	2	5	3	3	2	2	4	3	4	1		80
0900–1000	2	1	2	1	4	1	5	6	2	5	4	3	5	3	4	2	5	4	6	4	3	3	4	5	4	3	2	4	2	3	2	101
1000–1100	5	4	8	4	3	3	3	6	7	4	5	4	3	4	6	2	2	3	5	3	1	1	2	3	2	3	4	2	5	2	3	107
1100–1200	2	2	3	4	5	3	2	3	3	4	2	5	1	2	2	5	4	2	1		4	3	4	2	1	3	4	2	3	2	3	86
1200–1300	2	1	1	3	2	3	3	3	1	3	3	4	2	2	1	5	5	1	4	3	2	4	3	7	2	3	3	2	2	1	3	81
1300–1400		2	4	5			5	3	5	4	3	2	3	1	5	1	3	3	3		2	1	2	6	3	1	4	3	1	4	2	78
1400–1500	2	5		4	4	1	3	1	5	5	1	2	1	2	2	4	1	2	5	1	4	3	1	4	5	1	4	1	1	5	3	77
1500–1600	1	7	2	6	2	5	4	4	4	1	2	1	3	3	2	2	4	4	3	2	1	2	5	5	1	2	4	2	4	3	3	80
1600–1700	2	2	1	4	1	5	2	6	2	3	3	2	1	1	2	5	6	6	2	1	6	2	2	3	2	4	1	1	1	2	6	81
1700–1800	1	2	2	2	5	6	1	4	1	5	3	3	3	1	4	2	5	2	1	2	2	1	3	6	6	1	3	3	3	3	2	85
1800–1900	3		3	2	1	3	2	1	4	5	2	5	4	3	3	2	1	3	3	2	3	4	4	2	3	1	2	2	5	5	6	82
1900–2000	2	1	3	4	3	2	1	3	2	2	2	1	4	3	1	1	1	3	2	4	2	1	2	1	2	3	1	2	3	2	5	64
2000–2100	3	4	5	4	3	3	6	3	4	5	4	4	5	3	5	3	3	1	3	2	1	4	3	3	3	3	3	1	2	3	2	84
2100–2200	2	2	2	3	3	3	2	3	4	2	5	2	2	3	3	1	2	3	1	4	1	3	3	2	3	1	3	2	1	2	4	70
2200–2300	2	4	2	1	2	2	1	3	4	4	2	4	1	2	3	4	2	2	2	3	2	2	3	4	4	2	3	3	3	5	3	75
2300–2400	3	2		2	1	1	2	1	1	2	1	1	1	2		3	2	1	2		1	3	3	1		2	1	1	2	2	1	37
Total	38	46	49	51	46	46	40	44	58	57	46	54	40	44	46	55	60	50	56	35	39	54	55	53	53	34	52	38	51	56	61	
	F	S	S	M	T	W	T	F	S	S	M	T	W	T	F	S	S	M	T	W	T	F	S	S	M	T	W	T	F	S	S	

27

never work weekends. Two always have to work days. Finally, three of her nurses need to work nights because of family constraints. Fortunately only one of these special cases is a Triage nurse, and he is one of the three who requests to work nights.

As Gayle sits down at her desk, yesterday's memo from Roberto Sanchez, the Chief Administrator of the hospital, catches her attention. "I'll have to get to this memo as soon as I am done with the schedule. This is important. If we're going to remodel or expand ER, I want to make sure we're working from the right information!"

Lower Florida Keys Health System

M E M O R A N D U M

To: All Department Directors
From: Roberto Sanchez
Date: May 15, 1992
Subject: Facility Planning

As you may be aware, we are beginning a major remodeling/ expansion program here at LFKHS. The first stage of this program is a needs assessment investigation. I am asking all of you to take a careful look at the true capacity of your unit, to estimate the expected demand for the next year, and to make recommendations for what we should do to best meet your needs. If possible I would like your analysis and recommendations by June 3, 1992. If you have any questions, please stop by and ask.

As in other parts of the hospital, the number of beds is the generally agreed upon measure of capacity. ER currently has nine beds. However, many of the patients admitted to ER are not actually in ER all the time. If they require X-rays, they have to go down the hall. About 35% of the patients require X-rays, and it takes about 40 minutes for a typical X-ray. Further, not all patients in ER require beds. The Fast Track patients and some of the category 3 and 4 patients can be treated at the nurses' station and sent back to the waiting room. Patients who don't require beds make up about 25% of the patients who come in to ER. Finally, in times of really high demand, patients can be put in the hallway outside ER on gurneys or in wheelchairs. Gayle would rather not do that but will. Her goal is to maintain the safety and health of the patient, but she can put three patients in the hallway if absolutely necessary.

The average length of stay in ER is three hours for those patients who are treated and released. This includes the 20 minutes or so it usually takes to get a patient processed and into a bed. Of course this varies considerably, with some patient stays being much longer, some being much shorter. On the average, a nurse will be attending a patient about 40% of the time he or she is in ER. Nurses generally perform certain basic tasks, such as taking temperatures or blood pressure, while waiting for the doctor. They assist the doctor with the examination and complete any paperwork necessary for treatment of the patient. If the patient has to go to X-ray or the lab, an orderly handles the transportation. This frees up the nurse, but not the bed space, to attend to another patient. A certain amount of time is also spent just waiting for different services. Because of this slack time, nurses can generally handle two patients at a time.

Although a three-hour average stay is an improvement over last year's numbers, Gayle would like to see 75% of all the patients out in two hours or less. Each patient who comes into ER typically receives service from more than one person. Gayle has worked very closely with her people and the other areas of the hospital, primarily X-ray and the lab, to reduce the waiting once the patient has actually been admitted. There isn't a great deal of it now, and there will be less.

Each bed in ER is allocated about 60 square feet of floor space, though this can be somewhat flexible. The beds are in one large ward and are separated by drawn curtains. This allows the nurses and other caregivers to move freely and quickly between patients. Sometimes, however, all the beds are filled. This is the biggest hurdle Gayle faces right now in reducing the total time a patient is in ER.

"As far as the request for a needs assessment," Gayle thought as she set the memo next to her schedule worksheet, "I have some specific ideas about equipment and materials needed to improve the ER operations. I can cover those in the next day or two. As soon as I've completed the schedule, I'll have to come up with some accurate numbers for the capacity of the Emergency Room."

CASE 3　　　Lower Florida Keys Health System: Inventory and Purchasing

"We're out of what?" Dan McCooey asked his assistant. "Well, take the usual steps. Ask the Charge Nurse if there is a substitute we can supply until we restock. Fortunately it's only a sterile dressing package, and we know there are usually good substitutes." As his assistant walked away, Dan shook his head knowing these stock-out situations happened far too frequently. He resolved to eliminate this problem once and for all.

He knew the root cause of the problem. The computer system the hospital uses for inventory doesn't reduce the on-hand amount by withdrawals. It *records* both additions to and withdrawals from inventory, but it doesn't make the adjustment. "Only the government could buy an inventory control system like this one," Dan thought. "The one I had over at DePoo didn't have this problem." He picked up the phone and called Ruth Smith, the Assistant to the Administrator. "Ruthie, is Roberto in today? Great, can you put me down for about thirty minutes this afternoon? Three is fine, I'll be there. Tell him it's about the computer system." As he put down the phone, he made a note that he would have to prepare a quick proposal for this meeting. "We've got to do something about this computer system soon! It's costing us money."

Dan McCooey is the Director of Materials Management at the Lower Florida Keys Health System's (LFKHS) hospital. He held a similar position at the privately owned DePoo Hospital before it merged with the county-owned Key West Memorial. The LFKHS was established as a result of the merger. Many of the formerly separate functions, Materials Management being one, were combined into one new centralized

31

function in the reorganization. Like the other people who came over from DePoo, Dan inherited Key West Memorial's existing systems and procedures. In this case, that included a very peculiar computer system. But it also included a pretty good system for stocking the individual departments.

Several of the departments have an exchange cart system in place. These carts are essentially mobile stockrooms. Each day the old cart is wheeled down to the Central Supply Room (CSR) and exchanged for a new, fully stocked cart. The old cart is then replenished to be ready for the next day. The amount and type of stock on each cart is a function of the requirements of the individual departments. Table 1 is an example of the type of material on a cart. Dan's group has kept records of usage so these carts are well suited to the actual department requirements. The only adjustments come during the summer when levels are reduced by as much as 50%. The number of patients in the hospital is highly seasonal with winter being quite a bit busier than summer. Dan's people make the adjustment when they see the replenishment requirements dropping off.

Sometimes a department will request a change in stocking levels. "I just got one yesterday from the second floor," Dan thought. "It's for a mix of 24" x 1", 20" by 1 1/4", and 18" by 1 1/4" catheters. They have been using about 1100 of these each year and want their cart quantity increased from 3 of each to 6 of each." When a department asks for a change in any of the items or quantities, Dan usually does an EOQ analysis of the stocking level on the cart to see if the change makes any sense. He is not sure that this is the right approach, though. The minimum total cost approach of EOQ analysis makes a lot of sense on the surface, but Dan wonders if this is right for a hospital.

A few of the departments, those with space available for permanent storage areas, fill out an inventory worksheet each day and bring the form down to the CSR. Based on the inventory worksheet, the CSR clerks assemble the requested material to be picked up later. The inventory worksheets have a list of items and desired maximum stocking levels preprinted to make inventory level review, ordering, and order filling easier. The stock-up-to levels on these worksheets are determined using the same recordkeeping system as the carts. Table 2 is one of these worksheets from the third-floor nursing station. Both of these systems seem to work pretty well, and they are both very common in the health care industry. "This is certainly better than the old days when anybody could send out a PO," Dan reminisced. "They passed them out like party favors. Today that could get a person fired!"

TABLE 1 Basic Surgery Cart

Par	Used	SKU		Par	Used	SKU	
			Disp. linen				**Catheters**
4	——	375	100 Minor Pack	5	——	1245	Angiocath 20x1 1/4
4	——	362	131 Lap Pack	5	——	1247	Angiocath 18x1 1/4
4	——	315	410 Lg. Gown	5	——	1258	Angiocath 24x1
3	——	316	440 Xlg. Gown	10	——	1214	IV Start Pack
5	——	324	8376 Table Cover				
5	——	309	8355 Sm. Sheet				**Sponges**
5	——	310	8346 Lg. Sheet	20	——	546	Kerlix Sterile fluff
				10	——	534	Bulk Gauze 16-ply 4x4
			Gloves	25	——	537	Bulk Gauze 8-ply 2x2
4	——	258	Spectra size 6	25	——	581	Sponge Lap 18x18
4	——	259	Spectra size 6 1/2				
4	——	260	Spectra size 7				**Solutions**
4	——	261	Spectra size 7 1/2	1	——	2131	Ancef 500mg/50ml
4	——	262	Spectra size 8	1	——	2256	Dopamine in D5W 400mg/250ml
4	——	287	Eudermic size 6				
4	——	288	Eudermic size 6 1/2	1	——	2187	Heparin sodium/NSS 0.9% 1MU/50ml
4	——	289	Eudermic size 7				
4	——	290	Eudermic size 7 1/2	1	——	2062	Lidocane/5% dext IV/Viaflex 0.4% 18x500ml
4	——	291	Eudermic size 8				
			Instruments	1	——	2014	Dextrose in 1/2 saline 5% 1000m
1	——	913	Major set A				
1	——	915	Major set B				

(continued)

TABLE 1 (continued)

Par	Used	SKU	Item	Par	Used	SKU	Item
1	——	918	Major set C	1	——	2010	Normal saline 0.9% 1000m
2	——	926	Minor set A				
2	——	923	Minor set B				
6	——	952	Curved Hemostats				
3	——	987	Deaver Retractors				
8	——	947	Blade size 11				
8	——	949	Blade size 15				
8	——	941	Blade spear round				
9	——	968	Long Rt Angle Clamps				
5	——	671	Long Needle Holder				
4	——	674	Ribbon Retractor				
15	——	901	Softjaw Spring Clips				

TABLE 2   Floor Inventory Worksheet.

LOWER FLORIDA KEYS HEALTH SYSTEM

ISSUE WORKSHEET

6/22/92 ITEM NO.	DESCRIPTION	VEND/ITEM	LOC	PAR	3615 NURSING SERVICES	
					REQUEST	ISSUE
2048	SOLN, SODIUM CHLORIDE 1000ML	100310	SH1	3	—	—
151	BASIN, EMESIS DISP	121620	SH1	6	—	—
152	PAN, FRACTURE BED DISP	121650	SH1	3	—	—
153	URINAL W/COVER	121670	SH1	6	—	—
254	GLOVE, SINGLE UNSTERILE	106340	SH2	10	—	—
509	SPONGE, EZ PREP	107900	SH2	20	—	—
634	BANDAGE, KERLIX 4 1/2 STR	142360	DR1	4	—	—
621	BANDAID 1X3	142123	DR1	4	—	—
622	CLOSURE, SKIN 1/4X4	142110	DR1	5	—	—
624	DRESSING, ADAPTIC NON-AD 3	142750	DR1	5	—	—
686	BANDAGE, ELASTIC 4	142340	DR1	2	—	—
787	KLING, 2, STERILE	150175	DR1	2	—	—
790	KLING, 3, STERILE	150176	DR1	2	—	—
567	GAUZE, SPONGE STRIP 4X4 12PL	117420	DR1	10	—	—
570	APPLICATOR COTTON TIP	117890	DR1	10	—	—

"We rarely have a problem with the carts or the worksheets in the CSR," thought Dan. "The problem comes in the warehouse! It's like Goldilocks and the Three Bears back there. The inventory level is either 'too high' or 'too low'; seldom is it 'just right.'" Part of the problem, of course, stems from the computer system. Dan's staff has been trying to follow inventory transactions manually by calculating the on-hand amounts whenever items are removed or added to inventory, but many errors are made. Despite this problem, purchasing and the receipt of materials and supplies may be the biggest obstacle to managing inventory levels and maintaining a uniformly high level of service.

The LFKHS is located in Key West at the southernmost tip of the Florida Keys. It is 130 miles from Miami, and it is the largest hospital in the Keys. There is a smaller hospital, Fisherman's Hospital in Marathon, about halfway between Miami and Key West. There is one road, US 1, from Miami to Key West. This two-lane highway carries all the traffic for the Keys; commercial, tourist, and local. The only other practical form of transportation is by air. There is a nice, small airport in Key West with regular flights to Miami and other South Florida cities. However, this constrained transportation and relatively low level of demand means that the hospital suppliers in Miami do not give very fast service. For example, a large hospital in Miami might be getting supplies delivered twice a day from major suppliers. Even small hospitals can get essentially daily deliveries and 24-hour lead times. Even though its 100+ beds qualifies it as a medium to large hospital, LFKHS is lucky to get deliveries once a week. Dan figures the normal lead time for supplies is 10 to 12 days.

Dan has negotiated contract prices with several vendors for many common items. For example, he has a contract with one supplier for gowns. To get this price, however, he must order a fairly large quantity and allow a ten-day lead time. In many cases, he can't wait the ten days or can't justify the large order at the time the gowns are required. So he goes to a different supplier who will ship smaller quantities with a five-day lead time but at a higher price. The total vendor base for the hospital is about 45 frequent vendors and an additional 350 or so occasional vendors. Given this many suppliers, many carrying the same materials, it's usually possible to find one that will expedite an order. It is, however, costly and disruptive to go through this process.

While gowns are a simple example, this lead time problem occurs with many other supplies, some far more important. When there were two separate hospitals in town, DePoo and Key West Memorial, they could and did borrow from each other in the short run. They may have been in competition with each other for business, but patient needs

TABLE 3   Aggregate Inventory Analysis

Item	Family	Annual Amount	Number of Items
1	Anesthesia and hypodermic supplies	$ 333,297	269
2	Bulb	48,096	84
3	Catheters	139,225	96
4	Dietary	314,734	152
5	Disposable linen and operating room packs	879,229	246
6	Pharmaceutical supplies	107,161	100
7	Forms	321,484	800
8	Housekeeping and maintenance	311,358	112
9	IV supplies	467,460	198
10	Laboratory supplies	864,041	493
11	Medical/surgical	2,691,689	1,424
12	Office supplies	179,727	828
13	Parts	11,813	336
14	Patient care	56,534	57
15	Radiology	930,700	226
16	Surgical dressing and material	600,778	622
17	Sutures	180,571	256
	Total	$8,437,898	6,300

always came first. Now that the two have merged and there is only one central inventory for both facilities, they can't act as backup for each other. Fisherman's is simply too far away and too small to provide the kind of backup needed.

The solution in the past has always been to simply have lots of inventory. Currently the hospital carries about $900,000 worth of inventory. There are 6300 different SKUs (stock keeping units) divided into two different categories, regular (about 2800 SKUs) and surgical (about 3500 SKUs). Currently there is about $300,000 worth of regular inventory and $600,000 worth of surgical inventory.

Part of the reason that the surgical inventory is so much higher than the regular inventory is due to the exotic nature of some of the items. For example, if a hip replacement is scheduled, a hip replacement kit has to be ordered. The kit may contain only fifteen basic items, but each item comes in several different sizes. Often the actual sizes of things like screws and bolts can only be determined during the surgery. So the total kit may contain over 200 pieces. Many of these will be returned to the vendor after the surgery.

Contributing to the higher surgical inventory, and complicating its management, is the fact that much of the surgical inventory is subject to doctor preference. For any particular item, a catheter, for example, different doctors like different vendor's products. Thus not only does the item have to be stocked, but each doctor's preferred model of the item has to be stocked. Because of this doctor preference factor, and because of the highly specialized and sophisticated nature of the surgical inventory, Dan has delegated control of this material to Glen Sikes, Director of Surgery. Since Glen works with the doctors on all the scheduling and resource requirements for surgery, it makes sense for him to handle the surgical materials as well.

The regular inventory is much less exotic. It includes things like gowns, sterile dressings, catheters, IV bags, saline solutions, and other routine items. Table 3 summarizes the hospital materials purchases, including costs and annual usage of the items. Although a certain portion of the surgical inventory is treated as dependent demand, for example, ordering a hip replacement kit for a particular patient, all the regular inventory are treated as independent demand items. The major reason for this orientation is that each patient and each procedure is treated as unique. This makes it very difficult to establish anything like a list of common end items from which a dependent demand schedule could be developed.

The hospital inventory has no formal prioritization system. Dan does have a somewhat arbitrary classification system based on the "importance" of a particular item to patient care, but this is a very informal system. Further, costs are not included in this analysis. The stock is reviewed more or less continuously, and orders are placed when the stock gets low. The system is very imprecise, relying on the judgment of the people in the warehouse. Dan's office places all orders, even for the surgical items.

"Things have clearly improved over the past few months," Dan thought as he walked back into the warehouse, "but there is more to be done. Reducing the amount of inventory is the next step. With less to manage, there should be fewer errors. It seems as though there are three or four possible approaches to reducing inventory. I can reduce my order quantities, reduce the variability of my lead times, reduce the work-in-process inventory, or do a better job of matching ordering to demand. Of course, to do a better job of matching ordering to demand, I'll have to have better information about demand or do a better job of anticipating it."

Dan was still bothered by a special order that he had received from Glen yesterday. One of the doctors had just seen a new type of permanent dialysis catheter and wanted to implant it in a patient scheduled for surgery this afternoon. The hospital does not have an account with the company that makes the catheter, so it had to be shipped COD overnight. If things go according to schedule, the catheter will arrive one hour before surgery. "Of course, you have to do what's best for the patient, but with a little advance planning I could have saved a lot of money on this purchase. And, I could have been sure that the catheter is here before the surgery." The more he thought about it, the more Dan concluded that, "The real question is whether I can provide the same service level with less inventory at a lower cost. I think it can be done."

On the way back to his office, Dan's thoughts turned to a report sitting on his desk. A few weeks ago he had asked for an itemization of the

---

Lower Florida Keys Health System

M E M O R A N D U M

To: Dan McCooey, Dir. - Materials Mgt.
From: Jim McGonnell, Sr. Accountant
Date: July 9, 1992
Subject: Inventory Cost Analysis

Per your recent request, the information below represents the current cost structure for common inventory and purchasing decisions. Please note that these figures should be considered estimates since calculating the exact value of any of these numbers is problematic at best. However, these should be satisfactory for the planning activities you outlined in our last discussion. If you have any questions, please give me a call.

Order costs

Standard Floor Inventory Worksheet	$50
Average Floor Exchange Cart	$65
PO to an external vendor	$90
PO to an external w/expedite	$175

Holding Cost

As a percentage of the value
of the item(s) based on current
interest rates   22%

cost structure of typical inventory decisions. This was just completed yesterday. Sitting down in his chair, he spread the printout across the desk and began to examine the figures. "I'll need some of this information for my meeting with Roberto this afternoon. But maybe there are some answers in here for some of my other problems," he thought. "At least there ought to be some good questions."

COMPANY

MORRIS VALLEY ESTATE WINERY

CASE **1** : Strategy, Quality, and Productivity

CASE **2** : Forecasting and Purchasing

CASE **3** : Capacity, Scheduling, and Project Management

CASE 1

Morris Valley Estate Winery: Strategy, Quality, and Productivity

Jim Morris sat at his desk and let his gaze wander over almost 300 acres of vines. "Even though it's been a very dry summer," he thought, "the vines look great! This has been the best test so far of the buried irrigation system, and it has passed. Of course, the real test will come when we harvest the fruit and Cathy turns it into wine." Jim Morris is the son of one of the founders of Morris Valley Estate Winery in the Alexander Valley of northern Sonoma County, California. He has been the manager of Morris Farms since they started serious grape production about 12 years ago. He has brought an innovative spirit to the farming operation that is quite different from his peers in the area. The grape growers in Northern California are a very conservative group of people when it comes to managing their land. They do not easily integrate changes into their farming operations. For products as steeped in tradition as wine, this is in general a good idea. The history of wine production goes back many centuries, and the methods and lessons of its past are very important to the winemakers and wine consumers of today.

Wine making is really two completely separate operations. The first is the farming. At Morris Farms, Jim has about 400 acres under cultivation in three locations around the valley. Most of the fields are in the flat land bordering the Russian River. In these fields Jim has planted the Chardonnay, Sauvignon Blanc, and other similar vines. Two smaller hillside plots are reserved for the Cabernet. The interaction between the terrain and the Cabernet grape seems to impart a special quality to the fruit from those vines. The winery and Jim's office are located at the edge of Alexander Valley Road overlooking the 300 or so acres of the river bottom land. Figure 1 is a map of the area highlighting Morris Farms and the winery. Planting the fields, tending the vines, and harvesting the fruit at just the right moment are all critical operations. The farming provides the vital raw materials to the wine-making process. No matter how capable the winemaker, you must first start with good fruit. The second part of the process is the actual wine making. Morris Valley has a very talented young winemaker, Cathy Tharlson, who takes the fruit and turns it into fine wine. Their signature wine is a Fumé Blanc that is regularly recognized as one of the outstanding products of the area. They also make a Chardonnay and a Cabernet Sauvignon, all of which they sell in the premium wine market at retail prices starting at $10 and up.

Wine making is a relatively simple process on the surface, but making great wine takes a very special blend of both art and science. The production area of the Morris Valley Winery is shown in Figure 2. The harvested fruit is delivered to the crusher where the juice is extracted and the seeds, stems and leaves are filtered out. The juice is pumped into large stainless steel tanks where yeast is added to start the fermentation. For the white wines that are the specialty of Morris Valley, fermentation takes about ten months. Some of the wine remains in the tanks for the entire period, but some is aged in oak barrels. The oak im-

Figure 1   *Morris Valley Area Map*

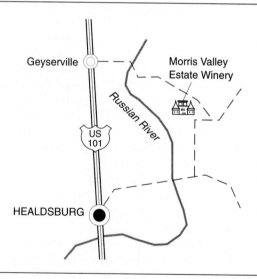

Figure 2 *Morris Valley Estate Winery Layout*

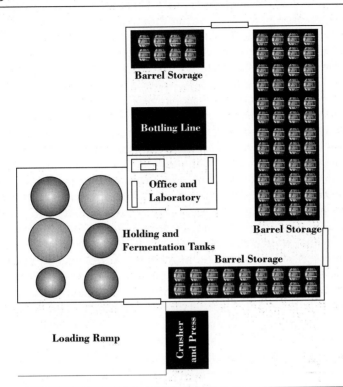

parts a special character to the Reserve Fumé. After fermentation, the wine is filtered to remove any remaining yeast and sediment and is bottled for distribution. In 1991 the winery installed its own small bottling line. Prior to that, the bottling was done by a mobile unit that services many of the small wineries in the area.

Above all else, quality is the most important aspect of the business. Every change made to the farming or wine-making operations has to at least maintain the same quality of product, if not improve it. Quality, however, is very difficult to define. Certainly the chemistry of the fruit is very important. Grapes must have the right amount of sugar, the right pH, and the right amount of acid to make great wine. Further, the ratio of pulp to skin must be in a certain range. Quality seems to be a function of the soil type, the climate, the watering, pruning, the type of vine, the terrain, the type of root stock, and other variables less easily defined or controlled. Yet, even if all of these variables are the same, two different plots of land may produce quite different fruit in the same year. It is a complicated process and even though grape growing in California has been going on for well over 100 years, consistently growing high-quality fruit remains as much an art as a science. Thus the tendency among most growers is to leave well enough alone. If things are going well, they don't make any changes. Even when things are going poorly, most growers are reluctant to make any major changes.

The Morris Farms operations have been very successful over the past few years (see Table 1). But they continue to look for ways to improve. About seven years ago, Jim started the installation of a buried drip irrigation system he discovered in South Africa. Virtually all the wine grape farms in Northern California use the traditional above-ground drip system. With this system the irrigation lines are strung along the vine trellises and the water drips down to the ground more or less continually during the growing season. The actual rate is carefully controlled to provide the desired amount of moisture for the fruit. The biggest problem with a traditional drip system is that water puddles on the surface instead of soaking down to the roots. This results in a micro-climate on the surface that can damage the vine.

A buried system is installed several inches underground and provides a much more efficient and direct source of irrigation. There is no evaporation loss or excessive water accumulating on the surface. Further, the buried lines are protected from accidental damage from farm equipment passing through the rows. The need to pass tractors and mechanical harvesters through the fields is why the standard is to leave 12 feet between rows of vines. Jim started with a small test plot, about 3 acres, and carefully monitored the results. They were excellent. The yield went from the old average of 3.75 tons of fruit per acre to about 4 tons per acre. This was a considerable improvement over the acreage using the traditional irrigation system and the quality of the fruit was at least equal to the other plots. It also seemed clear that the number and size of clusters each vine developed was more consistent in the test plot than in other fields. He has added more and more acreage each year, and by 1988 virtually all of the 300 acres of bottom land had buried irrigation installed. The results continue to be excellent.

The buried drip system is a little more complicated than an above-ground system. Installation requires a trench be dug perhaps 18 inches down and the tubing laid in the trench. Underneath each vine, vines are generally planted 8 feet apart, an emitter is spliced in the tubing to allow the water to flow into the soil. Once the system goes in the ground, maintenance is very difficult, so considerable care must be taken during

TABLE 1 Morris Farms Farming Operations. Summary Balance Sheet, 1988–1992

Revenue	1988	1989	1990	1991	1992
Sales	$1,053,864	$1,041,318	$1,129,140	$1,179,324	$1,254,600
Interest	1,106	1,120	1,246	1,260	1,400
Total	$1,054,970	$1,042,438	$1,130,386	$1,180,584	$1,256,000
Expenses	**1988**	**1989**	**1990**	**1991**	**1992**
Direct Labor	$122,724	$131,595	$137,510	$140,467	$147,860
Irrigation	74,080	75,592	94,252	80,417	86,470
Nursery Stock	2,400	2,460	2,850	2,910	3,000
Equipment Rental	1,342	1,373	1,404	1,466	1,560
Chemicals	84,242	85,210	87,147	91,020	96,830
Housing	993	1,218	1,245	1,271	1,324
Repairs	3,129	3,166	3,464	3,613	3,725
Taxes	376,004	389,930	417,782	436,350	464,202
Capital & Equipment	7,000	62,000	18,000	3,000	10,000
Depreciation	12,308	13,571	14,360	14,991	15,780
Administration	146,832	140,233	151,782	160,031	164,980
Maintenance	5,867	5,937	6,496	6,775	6,985
Insurance	794	853	882	941	980
Utilities	3,455	3,583	3,881	4,009	4,265
Total	$831,054	$906,348	$929,795	$935,536	$995,731
Net Profit (Loss)	$223,916	$136,090	$200,591	$245,048	$260,269

the installation. Further, a plugged emitter presents a real problem. For that reason, a fairly sophisticated filter system is installed to clean the irrigation water before it is pumped into the buried system. The tubing costs $0.05/foot, each emitter is $3.00, and the system costs $150/acre to install. The filter system is centralized and can supply water for the entire system. It costs $3500 installed.

The buried irrigation system is just part of Jim's approach to managing the farming operations. He is always looking for ways to improve productivity and quality. Sometimes this requires capital investment. The buried irrigation system is one example. In another effort, Morris Valley built a bunk house for their workers a couple of years ago. By providing a place for the essentially migrant workers to live in reasonable conditions, Jim feels he can improve employee morale, retain good employees, and improve their overall productivity.

Some of the improvements, however, come through process improvement. His current interest is in pruning techniques. Jim classifies his vines into three basic categories by their vigor. Vigor is the enthusiasm the vines show in their growth. It is observed by the color and quantity of the leaves, the thickness of the stalks, and the quantity of fruit. The most aggressively growing vines are A vines and the least are C vines. The desirable situation is, curiously enough, to have virtually all B vines. This intermediate rate of growth provides the best balance of quantity and quality of fruit and consistently produces the best grape for the winery. The vigor of a vine is observed as the plant develops during the growing season. It becomes clear after the first few weeks of growth how the canopy is developing and what type of vigor the vine has. No matter how much care is taken in the selection, planting, and nurturing of the vines, some A, B, and C vines will always develop. There is no way to predict how an individual vine will turn out.

There is a mythology about grapes having to "suffer" as they grow in order to develop character. Jim and his father Lou do not agree. They liken this to starving a child and then expecting it to grow up healthy and well balanced. As Lou says, "A certain amount of interesting life is valuable to you. But you can get carried away with that just like anything else." A C vine does not exhibit enough vigor. It does not grow enough leafy canopy and, in general, develops less fruit. An A vine is just the opposite. It develops far too much canopy, blocking out needed sunlight for the fruit below. This type of vine also produces less fruit than it should. The B vines fall in the middle with a balanced amount of canopy and fruit. Currently Jim is getting 4 1/2 tons of Sauvignon Blanc fruit per acre from B vines and about 3 tons from the A and C vines.

Jim's challenge is to make C and A vines into B vines. He thinks he may be able to do this through the use of new pruning techniques.

To control the growth of a vine, it is necessary to continually prune undesirable new shoots that will detract from the vine's ability to produce the desired fruit. The pruning also shapes the canopy so that the right amount of sunlight reaches the grapes. There are about a dozen basic pruning methods, each with its advantages and drawbacks. Jim has been using one called the cane pruning method. In general, it has worked well. Last year, however, he developed a new method that looks quite interesting. It has two big advantages. First, it is actually simpler than the cane method he is now using. That means it will be easier to teach it to the workers he employs. Second, there is less room for error in this system than in the cane method. This point is very important.

The workers move quickly through the field pruning each vine as they go. In fact, each worker prunes about 40 acres per season. They cut off the undesirable new growths and leave the desired number of canes. This number varies from field to field, but it is usually between five and ten productive canes per vine. It can be relatively easy to make a mistake. A slip of the knife and a good cane is cut off along with a bad one. Now there is one less cane to produce fruit. If there were only five to start with, this is a critical problem. The vine has just lost 20% of its fruiting capacity. With the new system, the worker is much less likely to make a mistake. The new system is simpler, and the workers pick it up faster. The only question in Jim's mind is whether it works for all the vines or does it work well on some but not others. He knows that B vines will produce at the same level with the new system, but will it improve the C vines or tame the As?

To find out, he ran a test. For the past year he has used the new pruning system on a 20-acre block of Sauvignon Blanc. This block was very useful because it contained all three types of vines. There were about 10% A vines and about 15% C vines, the average for the entire farm. He kept very close watch on the fruit all year and everything seemed to go well. The workers certainly liked the simpler system, and Jim is in favor of keeping things as simple as possible. With crush just completed, Jim now has time to analyze the results. The 20 acres produced 82 tons of fruit. This was less than the field produced the year before under the old system. It had become obvious during the year that the C vines were not responding well to the new system. Jim estimates that the C vines only produced 7 1/2 tons of fruit, but the A and B vines seemed to do well. "Is this my imagination? Does the new system work? How can I tell from the information I have?"

As he got up from his desk chair to walk to the window overlooking the fields, his glance fell on the pile of mail awaiting his attention. On top was a flyer promoting a new book in the design of experiments for quality improvement. "I wonder," he thought as he picked up the flyer, "is this the tool I need to answer my questions?"

CASE **2**

Morris Valley Estate Winery: Forecasting and Purchasing

Cathy Tharlson was standing in the middle of the barrel storage area of the winery. "Well," she thought, "I've got all the Reserve and Cabernet in the barrels and the rest of the Fumé in a tank. Now it's time to figure out how many bottles and corks I'll need this summer." Cathy is the winemaker at Morris Valley. It is her responsibility to take the fruit Jim Morris grows on Morris Farms and turn it into premium wine. The winery is known for its excellent Fumé Blanc, a variation of Sauvignon Blanc. They make a regular Fumé and a Reserve. The major difference between the two is that the Reserve spends much more time in oak barrels than the regular Fumé. They also make a Chardonnay and a well-respected Cabernet Sauvignon.

Wine making is a relatively straightforward process, but making respected premium wines takes a very special blend of both art and science. The production area of the Morris Valley Winery is shown in Figure 1. The harvested fruit is delivered to the crusher where the juice is extracted and the stems and leaves are separated. The must (it's not yet real juice) then goes to a press where the skins and seeds are removed. The juice is pumped into large stainless steel tanks where any remaining solids are allowed to settle. This usually lasts one or two days. The clear juice is then pumped to another tank where it is cooled and yeast is added to start the fermentation. The initial fermentation process takes about one week. The regular Fumé remains in the tanks for about seven months until the Chardonnay is ready to come out of the barrels. The Fumé then goes into the oak barrels for the last three months of its development. The Reserve Fumé, the Chardonnay, and the

51

Figure 1   *Morris Valley Estate Winery Layout*

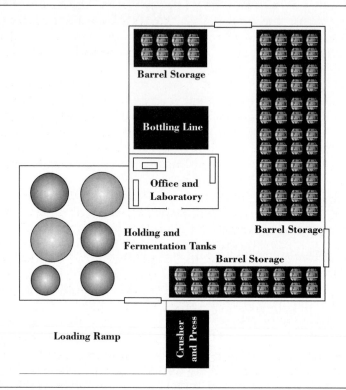

Cabernet are drawn out of the tanks right after the yeast is added. The Reserve and the Cabernet spend the whole fermentation time in barrels, but the Chardonnay finishes in the tanks. The oak barrels impart a special character to the wine. The Cabernet spends more time in the oak, up to three years. For the Fumé Blanc wines that are the specialty of Morris Valley, complete fermentation takes about ten months. After fermentation, the wine is filtered to remove any remaining yeast and sediment and bottled for distribution. In 1990 the winery installed its own small bottling line. Prior to that the bottling was done by a mobile unit that serviced some of the small wineries in the area.

The grape harvest usually occurs in late August and early September. Different types of grapes and different plots of land ripen at slightly different times, so the work in the winery is spread out over several weeks. Crush, the period of time when the fruit is harvested and the wine making starts, is aptly named. Not only do they crush the grapes, but the amount of work that must be done at the winery is staggering. When a field is ripe, the farmer may only have a day or two to pick the entire crop. The grapes then have to be processed quite quickly before their chemistry changes. Generally this means a winery will work 24 hours a day for several days.

The harvest this year was true to form. The Sauvignon Blanc grapes began to ripen in August and between the 16th and the 18th, Jim Morris had to pick as many as he could. He had to stop when the Chardonnay grapes reached maturity because they would not wait. The Sauvignon Blanc, as it happens, will. They have two flavor peaks, one early and one late. The Chardonnay grapes have only one peak. By August 21, the first round of harvesting was done.

As the grapes were picked, they were delivered directly to the winery for crushing. If they sit in the heat too long, their flavor and quality deteriorate. By August 22, Cathy had the first part of the 1992 harvest in the barrels. All of the Sauvignon Blanc fruit had gone to make Reserve Fumé and had been drawn into barrels, though some of the later harvest would also go to Reserve. The Chardonnay was all in and all in barrels. The winery could now return to a normal schedule until the rest of the harvest came in. By September 10, it was all over.

The harvest and crush had been successful. There were about 29,250 gallons of regular Fumé, 11,700 gallons of Reserve, 8600 gallons of Cabernet, and 21,000 gallons of Chardonnay. Cathy estimated this would ultimately result in between 29,000 and 30,000 cases of wine. Further, they had used up every barrel in the building. On the one hand, this was good. The winery wants to produce as much Reserve Fumé as possible, and Cathy was able to fill the barrels with the best wine. However, she had used quite a few more new barrels to do this than she would have liked. The Reserve gets part of its character by fermenting some of the wine in old barrels, and some in new. The new barrels create a stronger oak flavor and, when blended with the wine from the old barrels, create just the product Cathy wants. Having to use more new barrels than she planned means the wine will have a stronger oak taste this year. "I'll just have to wait to see how it turns out. I may be able to blend in some regular Fumé to soften the edge if it's necessary. But maybe I won't have to. You never can tell exactly how the wine is going to turn out in the end. It would be nice if I could get the number of new and old barrels right each year and then I wouldn't have this problem! It's not difficult to get new barrels, but a new barrel has to have held wine for at least six months before I can use it as an old barrel. I like to hold the amount of Reserve in new barrels to about 25%, but I can always put some Chardonnay in new barrels. You know, I have all the figures from the last four years (Table 1). I'll bet I can use those along with this year's numbers to figure out what I'll need for next year. But I bet I'll still have a problem with bottles!"

The Morris Valley Estate Winery is relatively small. It must buy all the same materials as a very big operation, but at smaller volumes. This creates some problems. One of the biggest problems is with bottles. To the bottle manufacturers, Morris Valley's order of 350,000 or so bottles a year is small potatoes. Unfortunately this means that the glass manufacturers assign Cathy's orders a very low priority. It is not uncommon for orders to arrive late, short, or of poor quality. Sometimes Cathy gets all three! Late isn't a huge problem, as long as it's not too late. The actual bottling operation can usually be delayed by a few days or a week with only minor difficulty. However, similar to crush, bottling tends to be done at all the wineries at the same time. This means that the part-time help Cathy needs to run the bottling line may not be available at other times. They might be working at other wineries. Thus late orders can cause some scheduling problems.

Short orders are another matter. Cathy has to get the wine out of the tanks and barrels and into bottles to satisfy the continually growing customer demand. If she is late getting a vintage to market, it could mean lost sales and lost customers. Therefore bottling must start in June. If the

TABLE 1   Morris Valley Estate Winery Barrel Usage Records, 1988-1992

Wine	1988	1989	1990	1991	1992
Fumé	431	447	473	511	532
Total Reserve	172	181	194	200	212
Reserve (old)	129	136	144	150	130
Reserve (new)	43	45	50	50	82
Chardonnay	305	328	340	328	376
Cabernet	124	133	137	147	156
Total Barrels in Use	1032	1089	1144	1186	1276
Total Barrels (old)	989	1044	1094	1136	1194
Total Barrels (new)	43	45	50	50	82
Unused New	0	0	0	0	0
Unused Old	26	5	0	8	0
Available Barrels	1058	1094	1144	1194	1276

bottle order is short, there will have to be a second setup when the remainder of the order arrives.

To compound the problem of small volumes, Morris Valley also uses a smoked bottle for all their white wines. They prefer this to clear or green bottles. Only two manufacturers in the U.S. make smoke wine bottles, and the lead time for an order is six months.

The quality issue is another matter entirely. In general, quality problems fall into two basic categories, bottle dimensions and bottle integrity. The bottles are supposed to be just the right size to hold 750 ml of wine when filled to just below the bottom of the cork. This is not always the case. Sometimes the bottles are too big. If Cathy puts just 750 ml of wine in the bottles, the wine will not fill far enough up the neck. Customers may feel they are being shortchanged, even though just the opposite is true. So Cathy adjusts the fill quantity so the level is right. But this means putting more than 750 ml in each bottle and, therefore, filling fewer bottles. Further, the ATF (Bureau of Alcohol, Tobacco, and Firearms) people from Washington are very narrow-minded about such things as fill quantities. If the bottle says 750 ml on the outside, it's supposed to have 750 ml on the inside. This is allowed to vary some, well under 10%, for two reasons. A short fill violates labeling laws and is unfair to the customer, but too much wine means the government is not getting all the excise tax to which it is entitled. As you might expect, the ATF auditors are much more concerned about too much wine than too little. However, there are other problems with bottle dimensions. If the inside diameter of the neck is too little or too big, the cork will not fit properly. If the neck is too big, the cork may leak. If it is too small, the cork insertion process on the bottling line may actually break the bottle. This creates a real mess and is a very expensive problem.

The integrity problems are less frequent but more dangerous than the dimension problems. Integrity problems can arise when the bottom of the bottle is not of a uniform thickness. If it is too thin on one side, the bottle will be weak and may break. This is a problem if it breaks during bottling, but an even bigger problem if it breaks in the hands of a customer. Cathy tries to find these bottles before they are filled and throw them away. Bottles can also have chips or cracks, and those must be discarded as well. Finally, a series of cosmetic problems may occur. The color of the glass may change from one end of the run to the other; there may be obvious mold lines; and there may occasionally be a "bird swing." This is a ribbon of glass that runs from one side of the bottle to the other inside the bottle! The biggest problem with poor quality is that if a problem doesn't show up until the bottling operation actually starts, it's too late to take any corrective action.

To try to find some of these problems early, Cathy opens and inspects one or two cases of bottles when the shipment arrives. If any obvious problems are visible, she has some chance to fix them before the bottling starts. However, some of the dimensional problems only seem to show up on the line. In all fairness, Cathy has noticed that quality does seem to be improving in the last few years. Table 2 summarizes the quality problems she has experienced in the past five years.

Cathy actually deals with glass brokers, not directly with the glass companies. The brokers try to make the process as painless as possible, but they can't do much about poor quality either. "Last year I was talking to Laura Gilbert, the glass broker, a couple of days before we were to start bottling. She asked if there was anything she could do to help. Well, we needed an extra hand to help us break down the cardboard shipping cases, so she came over." The winery distributes its products in special cases with the winery name and the type of wine printed on the sides in two colors. The bottle manufacturers will ship in special cases for big customers, but not for ones the size of Morris Valley. So Cathy has to take the twelve bottles out of each shipping carton, break down the carton, and pack the full bottles in new distribution cartons. She does reuse the internal dividers. "Not only did Laura come over and help break down about 1000 cases, but she brought chocolate chip cook-

TABLE 2   Summary of Quality Problems, 1987–1991

Problem Type	Number of Bottles				
	1987	**1988**	**1989**	**1990**	**1991**
Bad bottom	3972	4053	4094	4220	4306
Bird swings	31	31	31	32	33
Bottle too big	3361	3429	3464	3571	3644
Bottle too small	2139	2182	2204	2272	2319
Chips	3361	3429	3464	3571	3644
Color patches	1222	1247	1260	1299	1325
Cracks	611	623	630	649	663
Neck too big	1833	1870	1889	1948	1988
Neck too small	1558	1590	1606	1656	1689
Visible seams	5194	5300	5353	5519	5631
Weak color	7027	7170	7242	7466	7619
Total Defects	30,306	30,924	31,237	32,203	32,860

ies as well! I'm going to ask her back next time, even if I don't need the help."

In the past year, a Mexican glass manufacturer has been courting the wineries in California to try to generate new business. Cathy has been told that this past year they started producing a smoke bottle. "Chateau Corduroy was supposed to have used some of those bottles this past summer. I wonder how that went? It would be nice to have another supplier."

Bottles are not the only item that can create problems for Cathy. Finding good corks at a reasonable price is an ongoing struggle. In general, she feels the quality of corks is very poor, given how expensive they are. All natural cork comes from Portugal or Spain. Each factory or supplier grades the corks according to apparently completely subjective systems. Cathy has developed her own system which classifies corks into A, B, and C categories. An A cork is essentially perfect, a B cork has some imperfections, and a C cork is unusable. She looks for long cracks or chips that might cause leaks. Pieces of bad wood can also be a problem. The cork can be too hard and not compressible. Finally, she looks at cosmetic factors like holes and lines in the top.

She buys cork from local distributors. She visits their warehouse and pulls 50 or 60 corks from each bale she thinks might be satisfactory. A bale contains 10,000 corks. She visually inspects the sample corks and if the percentage of C corks is acceptably low, less than about 15%, she will mark the bale as a possible acceptance. She would like to have this percentage down around 10%, but that is tough to get in the current marketplace for the price she is willing to spend. She takes a few of the good corks from the bale back to the winery for testing. Poor-quality corks can taint the wine with an undesirable taste or odor. To test for this, Cathy places a sample cork from each bale under consideration in a small jar with a little wine and soaks them overnight. She uses an inexpensive white table wine that is neutral and doesn't have a lot of aroma so it will show the effect of the cork. If there is any contamination, the bale is rejected. If a bale is accepted, she places the order and has it shipped to the winery.

Just last year she had a big problem with an order. The lot that she received from France looked terrible. They didn't match the sample she had been given at all. Although they didn't leak, their appearance was unacceptable. She complained, and the owner of the company came out to try to resolve the problem. Neither Cathy nor the owner could find any lot, bale, or grade numbers on the corks. The shipment was, therefore, untraceable. Since price is a function of grade, the absence of this information was very important. Further, Cathy's invoice clearly showed lot and grade numbers. The owner's response was "Oh, that was the night shift. They screwed up." Needless to say, Cathy was not impressed. She ordered replacement corks from another supplier and told the owner to come and get his shipment. The changed plans cost a little more money because the replacement corks were a higher grade than Cathy normally buys as none were available in her normal grade.

This experience caused Cathy to think about alternate materials to replace the cork. "I know there are materials that are cheaper, more reliable, and better performing. One of these days I need to sit down with the Morrises and see what they think."

CASE 3

Morris Valley Estate Winery: Capacity, Scheduling, and Project Management

The post-crush planning meeting for 1992 was almost over. "Well, my friends, the winery has been good to us so far. Given the information you have all presented, what do we do next?" Lou Morris looked in turn at each of the other three people around the table waiting for their ideas. To his left was Henry Dengler, the other owner of the winery. Henry and Lou had started Morris Farms in 1979 as a wine grape farming operation only. Jim Morris, sitting across the table from his father, has run the farming from the beginning. In the early 1980s, they created the Morris Valley winery and brought out their first vintage in 1985. They decided from the outset to make and market premium wines that would, in general, retail for $10.00 per bottle and up. Cathy Tharlson, sitting on Jim's left, joined Morris Valley in 1987 as their winemaker. From the first vintage the wines have been very well received by critics, the press, and most importantly, the customers. In short, business has been going very well. Morris Valley has managed to maintain a continually growing sales volume even during the recent downturn in wine sales. They attribute this success to several factors.

The most important single aspect of their success is no doubt their complete commitment to maintaining the quality and integrity of the wine. Every decision made in the fields or in the winery must first maintain or improve quality. As they say, they enjoy life but are extremely serious about making outstanding wines. Of course, they are not the only winery in California that feels that way. However, unlike some others, they have been successful. Part of this is due to their willingness to experiment and adopt new technologies.

The wine-making industry is a very conservative business. Heavily steeped in tradition, most people are reluctant to make significant changes in either farming or wine-making processes. Given the nature of the premium wine market and the expectations of the customers, a certain amount of respect for tradition is a good idea. However, there is always room for improvement. Several years ago Jim installed a buried drip irrigation system in the Morris Farms fields and significantly improved both the quality and yield of the vines. Yet the other growers in the area still use the old above-ground system. This willingness to experiment and improve helps gain a competitive advantage in the marketplace.

Another aspect of their success has been their focus on premium white wines, especially Fumé Blanc and Chardonnay. In the past fifteen years, consumer preference has shifted from reds to whites, and this has helped Morris Valley. Their barrel fermented and aged Reserve Fumé is a particular success. Like most success stories, however, there are problems. The one facing the winery right now is capacity. The 1992 vintage used every bit of crusher, press, barrel, and tank capacity in the winery.

Making premium wines may be as much art as science, but the basic elements of the process are well understood. Figure 1 is a network flow diagram of the wine-making process as implemented at Morris Valley. This clearly shows the operations and time requirements to produce their four basic wines: Fumé Blanc, Reserve Fumé, Chardonnay, and Cabernet Sauvignon. The most critical time period in terms of winery capacity is during crush. In a very short period of time, hundreds of tons of grapes must be crushed and pressed to produce the juice that is held in tanks for up to several months. After fermentation is complete, the wine is put back in the tanks to be filtered and pumped to the bottling line. This again requires sufficient tank capacity. Figure 2 shows the current layout of the winery, including the tank locations and sizes and the barrel storage areas.

Crush lasts about two to three weeks generally from mid August to early September. During that period the winery must process all its fruit for the year. Grapes arrive from the fields in gondolas that hold about 2 tons of fruit each. The grapes are fed to a mechanical crusher that separates the stems and leaves from the fruit. The remaining material is called must, and it contains juice, seeds, pulp, and skin. The must is pressed to squeeze out the juice leaving the solids behind. This year Cathy rented a second press to supplement the one they own so that all the must could be pressed without having to be pumped into tanks. The juice is then pumped into holding tanks where it is allowed to settle for one or two days. The length of time the juice has to settle varies with

Figure 1   Network Flow Diagram of Wine Making Process

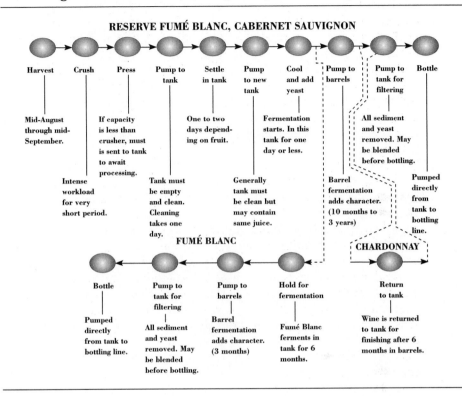

RESERVE FUMÉ BLANC, CABERNET SAUVIGNON

Harvest	Crush	Press	Pump to tank	Settle in tank	Pump to new tank	Cool and add yeast	Pump to barrels	Pump to tank for filtering	Bottle

Mid-August through mid-September.

If capacity is less than crusher, must is sent to tank to await processing.

One to two days depending on fruit.

Fermentation starts. In this tank for one day or less.

All sediment and yeast removed. May be blended before bottling.

Intense workload for very short period.

Tank must be empty and clean. Cleaning takes one day.

Generally tank must be clean but may contain same juice.

Barrel fermentation adds character. (10 months to 3 years)

Pumped directly from tank to bottling line.

FUMÉ BLANC

CHARDONNAY

Bottle	Pump to tank for filtering	Pump to barrels	Hold for fermentation		Return to tank

Pumped directly from tank to bottling line.

All sediment and yeast removed. May be blended before bottling.

Barrel fermentation adds character. (3 months)

Fumé Blanc ferments in tank for 6 months.

Wine is returned to tank for finishing after 6 months in barrels.

certain conditions. This year, for example, there was some wet weather at the end of August and some of the grapes developed mold. It takes an extra day to settle out the mold. At the very end of crush, Cathy had to hold up processing one day because she ran out of tank capacity. That one day made a difference in the fruit, and she had to allow an extra day for that juice to settle as well.

The timing of all this is quite critical. Grapes really cannot be harvested before about 7:00 or 7:30 AM. The dew has to be allowed to evaporate off the fruit. The capacity of the two presses Cathy uses totals about 5 tons, so she has to wait until that amount is in from the fields before she starts processing. She rarely starts crushing before 8:30 AM. Although she might have to wait for the fruit, it will not wait for her. As the grapes sit in the gondolas, heat builds. This is especially true of grapes picked in the afternoon or on very hot days. In fact, Jim often

Figure 2   *Morris Valley Estate Winery Layout*

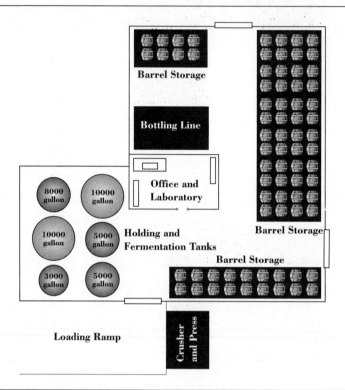

stops picking grapes by noon on warmer days. Heat causes a chemical change in the grape that has a noticeable negative effect on the wine quality. Therefore the grapes must be processed as quickly as possible. This wouldn't be a problem if Jim could simply leave them on the vines until Cathy was ready, but the fruit must come off the vine at exactly the right moment in order to obtain the highest quality. This might mean that a 20-acre field would need to be picked clean in a matter of a few hours! Fortunately the different wine grapes ripen at slightly different times. The Sauvignon Blanc and Chardonnay are usually first, with the Cabernet several days later. The log of the amount of fruit Cathy processed through the crusher this year is shown in Table 1.

The presses can process one cycle, that is, 5 tons of fruit, in about 1 hour and 35 minutes. It takes about five or ten minutes between press loads to clean and reset the presses and the cycle can start again. About

TABLE 1   Crusher Log – 1992

Date	Grape Type	Tons
8/16	Sauvignon Blanc	35
8/17	Sauvignon Blanc/	40
	Chardonnay	9
8/18	Chardonnay	45
8/19	Chardonnay	48
8/20	Chardonnay	40
8/21	Chardonnay	36
8/29	Sauvignon Blanc	35
8/30	Sauvignon Blanc	37
8/31	Sauvignon Blanc	30
9/1	Sauvignon Blanc	31
9/2	Sauvignon Blanc	30
9/3	Sauvignon Blanc	38
9/4	Sauvignon Blanc	40
9/5	Cabernet Sauvignon	36
9/6	Cabernet Sauvignon	37
9/8	Sauvignon Blanc	35

Notes: Fruit harvested on 8/29, 8/30, and 9/8 exhibited minor molding. Extra settling time required.

the maximum Cathy can crush and press in one day is ten press loads, or 50 tons of fruit. If she can start by 8 AM, the last load will be processed about midnight. Cathy employs two overlapping shifts of workers because she does not want anyone (but herself) to work more than twelve hours a day. She feels that too many mistakes start to happen after twelve hours, and mistakes can be really dangerous.

For example, if someone accidentally hooks up to the wrong tank, juices from different grapes could be mixed. This would probably cause the entire tank to be scrapped since premium varietal wines require essentially all of the juice to come from one type of grape. It is very important to keep different varieties and, on occasion, different batches, of juice separate. Although it might be possible to replace the juice, it is unlikely because contracts for fruit are signed months in advance. At any rate, the fruit will not be from Morris Farms and would likely be of a different, lower quality. This represents at least an extra materials cost and probably the loss of all revenues associated with the contaminated juice. Further, the crusher and presses themselves are quite dangerous. They each contain moving parts that can cause serious damage to hands, arms, feet, and other human parts not intended to be crushed or pressed. Tired people make mistakes, and Cathy doesn't want any of either.

Cathy feels that the 600 tons of fruit that the winery is processing now fully loads the available tank capacity and leaves no capacity cushion. That is the major problem she presented at the post-crush meeting. There is some urgency to dealing with this issue. Jim Morris reported that he expects the output of the farming operations to continue to grow at about 5% per year, and Lou and Henry want to see that fruit turned into Morris Valley wine, not sold to someone else. In fact, Jim would be willing to sell even more fruit to the winery if they could handle it. Currently about 150 tons of fruit that Morris Valley could be using is being sold to other wineries. It would take a couple of years to satisfy current contractual obligations, but eventually all of this fruit could go to Morris Valley.

Henry Dengler, other than being a partner, is a professional wine marketer. He supplies an annual forecast to the winery (Table 2). According to this forecast, the winery could sell more than it is capable of producing. The problem, then, is: Does the winery want to expand capacity and, if so, how and when?

Cathy was down in Rohnert Park last week at Rohnert Park Welding, the company that makes the stainless steel tanks. They have four

TABLE 2   Demand Forecast

Revenue (000)	1992	Actual 1992	1993	1994	1995
Sales	$ 1,299	$ 1,255	$ 1,344	$ 1,407	$ 1,479

Cases	1992	Actual 1992	1993	1994	1995
Fumé Blanc	13,659	12,305	14,081	14,771	15,781
Reserve Fumé Blanc	5,541	4,904	5,938	6,245	6,637
Chardonnay	9,045	8,697	9,135	9,478	9,554
Cabernet Sauvignon	3,933	3,608	4,150	4,376	4,676
Total	$32,178	$29,515	$33,305	$34,870	$36,648

Notes: 1992, 1993, 1994, and 1995 are demand forecasts and projected revenues. Actual 1992 is projected revenues based on actual barrels produced.

basic sizes, 3000 gallons, 5000 gallons, 8000 gallons, and 10,000 gallons, and they range in price from $13,000 to $47,000. Although all the tanks are custom made, delivery time is only about two to three months, depending on how busy they are. Most of the wineries in the area buy from this one company, and most seem to place their orders in the May/June timeframe. The tank would be delivered in September. By the time it is installed and the plumbing and refrigeration work completed, the tank would be ready for use in early November. At other times of the year, the delivery time is a few weeks shorter.

The tanks are delivered and installed by Sonoma Crane, which is right next door to Rohnert Park Welding. While she was there, Cathy stopped in to see about installation. Sonoma Crane had installed all the tanks at Morris Valley, so they were quite familiar with the layout. The good news was that a tank could be installed in the current tank room with minimal trouble and without relocating any major equipment. The bad news was that a 3000-gallon tank was all they could squeeze in.

Cathy wasn't sure a 3000-gallon tank would be enough. It might be fine for a couple of years, but then they would be in the same spot all over again. It might be a better idea to get an 8000- or a 10,000-gallon tank now. She asked the engineer from Sonoma Crane to come out and look the place over. She was interested in his recommendations for a new, larger tank installation. His report was a bit of a surprise.

Sonoma Crane's engineer recommended installing the tank outside the building where the crusher and presses were currently located. By moving them to a new location, the new tank could be installed right next to the others. The tank would have to be insulated, unlike the ones inside, and this added slightly to the installation cost, but the insulation would actually make the tank cheaper to refrigerate. A cover would have to be built over the tank to protect it from the sun and the elements, but Jim and the guys could do that for about $1000 in material.

A whole new concept opened up to Cathy. She had run out of barrel storage space in the winery last year and again this year. This is both inconvenient and expensive. They are currently storing 104 barrels in a local warehouse at a cost of $0.78/barrel/month. If they could move all of the tanks outside, she could free up the space for barrel storage. This would give Cathy space to store an additional 300 barrels. She asked Sonoma Crane to prepare an estimate of such a move, and she distributed copies of the one-tank installation estimate and the entire move estimate (Table 3) at today's meeting.

The plan has some significant problems. First, the tanks have to be empty to be moved. Scheduling this would be difficult. Except for the time right before crush, some of the tanks will always be in use. The

TABLE 3   Installation Estimate. Sonoma Crane, Rohnert Park, CA, Estimate, 9/29/92 (guaranteed for 90 days)

To install one new tank

Task	Tank Size (gal.)			
	3000	5000	8000	10,000
Load tank	$105	$ 125	$ 140	$ 165
Transportation to site	75	75	75	75
Unload tank	125	145	170	205
Install support bracing	160	200	225	270
Attach piping	50	50	50	50
Install refrigeration on tank	310	350	395	470
Apply foam insulation	NA	1,150	1,300	1,500
Site analysis & engineering	NC	NC	NC	NC
Total	$825	$2,095	$2,355	$2,735

Notes: Estimate does not include: the cost of relocating crusher and press, the cost of adding concrete pad space or permanent covering, the cost of running piping from new tank inside to existing tanks or connection to existing system, nor the cost of connecting new tank to current refrigeration system. Current refrigeration system can handle up to three additional 10,000-gallon tanks. If more than one tank is being insulated, Apply foam charges are reduced by $500.

To relocate six existing tanks

Task	Cost
Disconnect all piping and refrigeration	$ 300
Move six tanks to outside pad	1,200
Reinstall six tanks in new locations	750
Adjust and repair support bracing	550
Reconnect piping and refrigeration at tanks	400
Apply foam insulation to all six tanks	7,500
Total	$10,700

Notes: Estimate does not include: the cost of relocating crusher and press, the cost of adding concrete pad space or permanent covering, the cost of running piping from new locations to inside the winery or connection to existing system, nor the cost of purging and recharging refrigeration system. Each tank installation requires approximately one day.

move might have to take place in two or three phases. Second, the tanks are currently not insulated. When the winery was built, they decided to use the tank refrigeration to cool the barrel storage area as well. The cool tanks keep the barrel storage area at the desirable 50–55 degrees. By moving the tanks outside, cooling would have to be provided for the current building. Cathy hasn't had a chance to get a firm estimate on this yet, but the engineer from Sonoma Crane made an educated guess of $15,000 to $20,000 to install cooling for the winery. Finally, putting *all* the tanks outside would mean a much larger pad and roof than for one tank. There is also the issue of the complete disassembly and redesign of the piping system between the tanks and into the winery. Cathy and Jim have talked this over, and the winery has the people with the time and skills to do the roof and the piping if it can be done between January 10 and June 30. Cathy estimates the materials cost associated with this to be under $2500.

"This is obviously going to require some careful planning and management to get any changes made and not interrupt the business of the winery," Cathy thought as she turned to look out the window at the fields of now empty vines. "But I sure would like to be able to work with more of Jim's fruit. My wines will only be as good as the fruit I start with, and Jim's is terrific. What plan of action should I recommend?"

COMPANY

NORTHCOAST BANK

CASE **A** : Introduction to Operations Management

CASE **1** : Forecasting, Capacity, and Queuing

CASE **2** : Linear Programming, Integer Programming, and Scheduling

CASE **3** : Strategy and Location

CASE **A**

NorthCoast Bank: Introduction to Operations Management

"Maybe now they'll see that we have a real problem here. I could leave the ball in their court, but that hasn't worked well in the past. What should I do next?" Steve Pence thought about all this as he headed back to his office. Steve has been the President at NorthCoast Bank of Great Northern for six years. He had just come from a meeting with the building management where they had yet another discussion about the parking lot. Steve had tried to talk to the building manager before but was always put off when the manager dismissed his concerns as overreaction. The manager responded that he could see the parking lot from his office window and that he could always find a parking spot close to the door every time he looked out. Steve was forced to document the lack of parking space in order to make his point. He made a periodic visual check and maintained a log of his findings, complete with Polaroid pictures. These he had presented to the manager at their meeting.

The developer owns a substantial amount of vacant land adjoining the bank building. The building manager had talked about some potential plans for development of part of that land. They wanted to put in a strip mall with a video store, cleaners, restaurant, and so on. They had also mentioned the possibility of building a multistory parking garage, but cautioned that it was only a possibility at this time. Steve made the point that if the number of bank customers continued to grow at the current rate, the parking lot problem would worsen quite quickly.

NorthCoast Bank of Great Northern is located adjacent to a well-established shopping center in one of the larger suburbs of Cleveland. The bank occupies the main floor of a four-story office building. It is

71

bounded by a major artery on the north and parking lots on the south and east (Figure 1). Two ATM machines are located on the east side of the building adjacent to the access road to the shopping center. As is true of most suburban shopping centers, a good percentage of the parking area goes unused except during the holiday season. One of the tenants of the shopping center is a major savings and loan operation. Unlike NorthCoast Bank, they have a large drive-up area as well as a small traditional structure. To try to reduce traffic jams and waiting lines during peak times, they had even gone so far as to purchase existing drive-up banking facilities from a now defunct bank across the street from them. The experiment had not worked well and was soon terminated. In talking with new customers at the bank, Steve had learned that many of them were in fact prior customers of the S&L who had left because of the difficulty in transacting their business in a timely fashion.

The NorthCoast Bank started in 1963 with Roger Ringer as CEO and now Chairman of the Board. A holding company presides over all of the NorthCoast Banks. NorthCoast Bank of Great Northern is one of forty independently owned NorthCoast Banks operating in Ohio. It was founded in 1981 with $7 million in assets and now has $35 million in as-

Figure 1   *Area Layout*

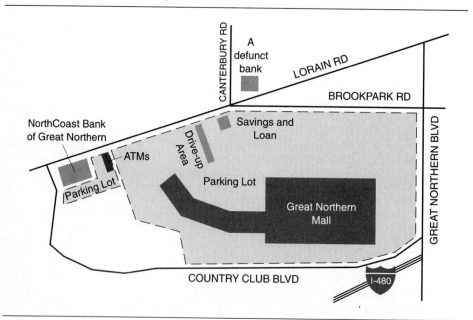

sets. NorthCoast Bank has centralized numerous functions such as check clearing, returned checks, and data processing. They also have mini-banks located in several of the local grocery stores. These mini-banks are considered to be branches of one of the stand-alone banks. NorthCoast Bank of Great Northern has responsibility for one of these branches at the Olmsted Falls Jordan's SuperMarket.

NorthCoast Bank considers itself to be a seat-of-the-pants operation. Its leaders believe in running a lean and innovative organization. They have no formal mission statement or published goals. They provide guidance to the bank presidents through bimonthly meetings, but give them the latitude to run their own show. In keeping with the corporate culture, there are very few levels of bureaucracy. Corporate decisions are made by holding company officers and then brought to the bimonthly meetings for discussion of implementation. These meetings also provide a forum for ideas that have come from the employees. In fact, the NorthCoast name was suggested by an employee and first presented at one of these meetings several years ago.

NorthCoast Bank of Great Northern is experiencing some growing pains, and something needs to be done soon or they could lose customers to the competition. The parking situation has become intolerable as the business of the bank and other tenants in their building continues to grow.

As Steve neared his office he could see Edith Hodge talking to one of the tellers, Kristin. Edith is the head teller at the Great Northern branch. Kristin has just asked Edith if it would be possible to not schedule her to work on Saturday for the next month. Scheduling gets to be a real nightmare for Edith because the bank is open Monday–Friday 9 AM–6 PM and Saturday 9 AM–12 Noon. Most people like to work a five-day work week and for budgetary reasons Edith must keep overtime to a minimum. Edith is charged with having enough tellers available to handle the demand while keeping staffing to a minimum. NorthCoast Banks have a policy of opening up an additional teller window if more than two customers are waiting in line. To have the right number of tellers available, Edith has to know how many customers to expect each hour of each day. Saturdays, Mondays, paydays, and lunch hours are peak times. Edith tells Kristin she will see what she can do and goes back to her desk to check schedules. Jan is on vacation this week and next. Laura is out with pneumonia, and Missy is working on a special project for corporate. Edith glances out the window at the two automated teller machines and just smiles.

Edith wondered where she was supposed to come up with another body to cover for Kristin. She had been pulling from the customer service area when demand was high, but with the opening of the Olmsted Falls Jordan's SuperMarket branch, that had become almost impossible. The mini-banks were designed to be minimally staffed. All phone calls for those locations were being handled by the customer service area of the parent bank.

Back in his office, Steve was reviewing the daily operating reports. He cringed when he saw that a data processing error had mistakenly credited a customer with a deposit of $17,520 instead of the actual deposit amount of $175.20. Fortunately the reconciliation found this error before the customer did, so it could be corrected during the overnight processing. "Boy," thought Steve, "I'd hate to see that go undiscovered until it shows up on a customer's statement. We'd have some pretty embarrassing explaining to do! That's not exactly the type of quality service we want to provide."

The results of the recent telephone survey were on his desk as well. They confirmed what Steve had believed all along. Of the calls coming into the bank, 80% were customer service calls. The next highest category was calls to officers. He glanced at his phone. All the lines were in use. This was rapidly becoming the norm rather than the exception to the rule. When they installed the telephone system, they thought they had allowed themselves plenty of room for growth.

Steve had recently moved the receptionist's desk back to the customer service area so that the receptionist could more easily see who was available to take customer calls. Customer satisfaction is one of the ways NorthCoast Bank measures the quality of its service. Steve was monitoring the monthly volume for incoming calls as well as the monthly charges for the 24-hour customer service lines. The system is currently set up so that if all of the Great Northern customer service lines are busy, a call automatically rolls over to the 24-hour customer service department. This seems to be working in the short run, but Steve isn't so sure about the long run. Some customers have expressed displeasure with not being able to speak personally with a customer service representative at Great Northern during regular business hours.

Early last year, in an effort to improve the quality of service being provided to the customers, corporate decided to implement a manned 24-hour customer service department. The idea was to make representatives available so that customers could get answers to their banking questions at any time of the day or night. NorthCoast Bank pioneered this concept in Ohio. The department is physically located in the North-Coast Bank Westgate building, but it is a totally separate operation with its own staff. Each NorthCoast Bank is charged a monthly fee allocated on a per item basis, depending on the volume handled by the 24-hour customer service operators.

The response to the service has been overwhelming. Calls are coming in at a rate of 60,000–70,000 per month. They have 43 lines dedicated to 24-hour customer service. They also use Westgate's 22 customer service lines when the bank is closed. When the service was first started, most of the calls were after hours as was originally intended. As customers became more familiar with the system, however, they started to call during regular banking hours as well. The number of daytime calls has increased so much that the operators have trouble handling the volume. They frequently have to transfer a call directly to the customer service department of the branch bank during peak demand. "We started this 24-hour phone banking to provide better quality service to our customers," Steve thought as he looked at his people busy on the phones. "I wonder if that's really what we are doing?"

As he prepared to go home, Steve reached for his boots and gloves. Only yesterday it had been sunny and 60 degrees—today there are 3 inches of snow on the ground. "Banking is not unlike the Cleveland weather," he thought. "What we are doing today will be totally different tomorrow. Responsiveness to customer needs is what it's all about."

CASE 1

NorthCoast Bank: Forecasting, Capacity, and Queuing

Early in April 1992, Lisa Stanley was working as a student intern at NorthCoast Bank of Great Northern located in the Great Northern Mall in North Olmsted, Ohio. As a senior at Case Western Reserve University majoring in Operations Management, she was hoping to gain some useful work experience and have a chance to practice some of the skills she was learning in her classes. Consequently she was pleased and somewhat excited when, on her second day on the job, John Homenko, the Vice President of Operations, called her into his office to ask her to take on a special assignment for him. John explained a little bit of the recent history of the bank's growth and the problem he wanted to assign her.

> We're one of 40 banks that are subsidiaries of NorthCoast Bank Holding Company of Ohio. Ten of these banks are very small operations located in grocery stores at various sites around Cleveland. The rest are located in their own buildings, mostly in the Greater Cleveland metro area. Thirteen of the banks are located around the northern part of the state outside of metro Cleveland. The "grocery banks" are part of a strategy we decided to try in 1987. It seems to be working out pretty well. The whole issue of our strategy in picking locations and deciding what services to offer is something you might enjoy investigating; but, for now, I have something else I'd like you to take a look at for me.

> The bank here at Great Northern was the thirteenth NorthCoast Bank to be chartered. It was one of three that started operations in 1981. We're not really very big—our assets are about $35 million—but we have a nice market niche here in this part of town. We've been seeing some modest but pretty steady growth over the last three or four years.

77

One of the areas in which this growth is being felt is in our teller operations. Right now we have twelve teller windows. Monday through Friday we have five full-time tellers and some part-timers. On Saturday we have eight tellers on duty.

I don't have any hard data, but it seems to me that, of late, there are more occasions when the lines at the teller windows are getting too long, especially at our busy times like at lunch and just before closing at six in the evening. Also, we seem to be having some trouble scheduling the right number of tellers at the right times. It's all right if we're a little over staffed at times because there are plenty of non-customer-related activities that the idle tellers can do: filing signature cards, filing loan documents, or helping out with some of the bookkeeping functions. If things get really backed up, we can get one of the people from "new accounts" to open a teller window and help out. Even the officers can pitch in to help (and they do). Everyone here can do teller duty.

I'm not even sure what I want to know. I guess I'm wondering if we need to hire more tellers? Or, will we need to do so in the near future? If so, when? How many tellers should we plan to have each day? How many at each different time of the day? I don't know what else we should be considering. What do you think?

Lisa and John discussed the matter for another fifteen minutes, during which time she learned that the five full-time tellers are normally scheduled to work 40 hours per week. They work four 9-hour days and one 4-hour day (usually Saturday). On Saturday and at busy times during the week, the full-timers are complimented by part-time tellers, some of whom work in other areas of the bank during the week, and some of whom work for NorthCoast Bank only on Saturday. As they went through this information, John wondered if a different schedule might be better. Lisa learned that the daily summaries of teller cash tickets were on file for as far back as she would care to look. Beginning with January 2, 1989, the daily totals were available in NorthCoast's computer files.

Before she left John's office, Lisa was able to confirm a number of things that she had already learned in her brief time at the bank. Customers waiting for tellers were divided into two lines, one for commercial customers and one for noncommercial customers. Usually one window is open for commercial customers, but at busy times, a second or even a third might be opened. "Noncommercial customers" includes people wishing to cash checks; exchange currency; make deposits or withdrawals to personal accounts; make loan payments; purchase money orders, cashier's checks, traveler's checks, etc.; and a variety of other transactions. Most, but not all, of the transactions involve cash (and, hence, were counted in the daily summaries). John speculated whether it might be better if they had only one line serving all types of customers. This would require some additional training because not all of the tellers were fully proficient at working the commercial lines. However, that would not present too much of a problem. When he mentioned that idea, Lisa speculated about whether it might make sense to go the other direction, toward more, not less, separation of customers of different types. There certainly were several ways in which such a separation could be done, if it were to be done at all.

A week following the meeting in John's office, Lisa sat down at her desk to consider what she had accomplished and what she wanted to do next. The day after her meeting with John, she had talked to the supervisor of bank security. He had agreed that it wouldn't be too distracting or too hard for his guards to count the number of people entering the bank who go to the teller windows. He talked with the guards and they agreed. So, for the next week they kept a log in which they recorded the number of customers entering the line for commercial teller window(s) and the number entering the line for noncommercial teller windows (see Table 1).

Lisa also had spent the better part of two days timing teller transactions with a stop watch. She had expected there might be a little resistance to her doing this, so she had been careful to get the proper clearances. After explaining the purpose of the project to the head teller

TABLE 1 Number of Customers Entering Teller Lines

Time	Commercial	Non-Commercial	Total
9:00 to 10:00	104	93	197
10:00 to 11:00	60	186	246
11:00 to 12:00	76	396	472
12:00 to 1:00	27	558	585
1:00 to 2:00	71	233	304
2:00 to 3:00	33	140	173
3:00 to 4:00	27	70	97
4:00 to 5:00	38	116	154
5:00 to 6:00	110	535	645
Total	546	2327	2873

Note: Figures are total number of customers for the five days April 13–17, 1992.

and answering her questions, Lisa had met with all the tellers (in two separate groups) to explain the project to them and to answer their questions. All had gone well, and she had gotten, she thought, some good data. After collecting the data, she developed a frequency table and a histogram. Then she decided to break the data down a little further. Since she had recorded the type and number of transactions each customer required, she was able to produce additional tables and histograms that, she hoped, might be useful (see Table 2 and Figure 1). In this breakdown, Lisa divided noncommercial customers into three categories: those making only a single transaction such as a deposit, loan payment, or cashing a check; those making multiple transactions; and those making transactions such as purchasing money orders, cashier's checks, or traveler's checks which normally take a long time and require the teller to leave the teller window.

TABLE 2   Distribution of Service Times. Composite of All Customers' Service Times

Service Time	Frequency	Relative Frequency	Cumulative Relative Frequency
negative	0	0	0
1 min. or less	122	0.325	0.325
1–2 minutes	74	0.197	0.523
2–3 minutes	33	0.088	0.611
3–4 minutes	35	0.093	0.704
4–5 minutes	31	0.083	0.787
5–6 minutes	31	0.083	0.869
6–7 minutes	17	0.045	0.915
7–8 minutes	11	0.029	0.944
8–9 minutes	13	0.035	0.979
9–10 minutes	2	0.005	0.984
10–11 minutes	2	0.005	0.989
11–12 minutes	4	0.011	1.000
12–13 minutes	0	0.000	1.000
14 or more min.	0	0.000	1.000
Total	375	1.000	

(continued)

TABLE 2 **(continued)** Distribution of Service Times

		Noncommercial		
Service Time	Commercial	Single Trans.	Multi- Trans.	Money Orders etc.
1 min. or less	0	116	6	0
1– 2 minutes	0	65	9	0
2– 3 minutes	4	20	9	0
3– 4 minutes	10	14	9	2
4– 5 minutes	11	10	8	2
5– 6 minutes	19	2	6	4
6– 7 minutes	11	3	2	1
7– 8 minutes	7	0	3	1
8– 9 minutes	9	0	3	1
9–10 minutes	2	0	0	0
10–11 minutes	0	1	1	0
11–12 minutes	2	0	1	1
12–13 minutes	0	0	0	0
14 or more min.	0	0	0	0
Total	75	231	57	12

Relative Frequency Distribution

		Noncommercial		
Service Time	Commercial	Single Trans.	Multi- Trans.	Money Orders etc.
1 min. or less	0.000	0.502	0.105	0.000
1– 2 minutes	0.000	0.281	0.158	0.000
2– 3 minutes	0.053	0.087	0.158	0.000
3– 4 minutes	0.133	0.061	0.158	0.167
4– 5 minutes	0.147	0.043	0.140	0.167
5– 6 minutes	0.253	0.009	0.105	0.333
6– 7 minutes	0.147	0.013	0.035	0.083
7– 8 minutes	0.093	0.000	0.053	0.083
8– 9 minutes	0.120	0.000	0.053	0.083
9–10 minutes	0.027	0.000	0.000	0.000
10–11 minutes	0.000	0.004	0.018	0.000
11–12 minutes	0.027	0.000	0.018	0.083
12–13 minutes	0.000	0.000	0.000	0.000
14 or more min.	0.000	0.000	0.000	0.000
Total	1.000	1.000	1.000	1.000

Figure 1 *Frequency Distribution Charts*

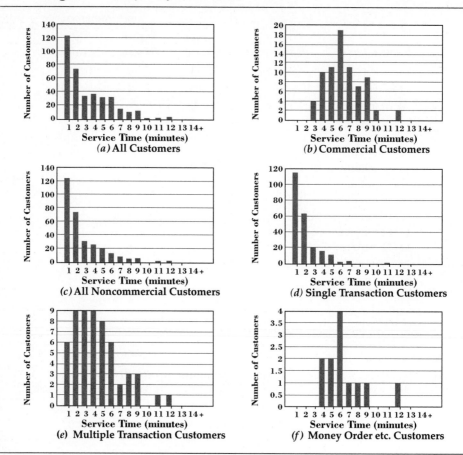

Finally, Lisa had accessed the data files with the daily summaries of teller cash transactions. From the more than three years worth of daily data, she had done some simple statistical analysis, consisting mostly of computing the average number of cash transactions per day. She had calculated the average for each month, for each day of the week, and for each date of the month. Since they would distort the normal patterns, she left the days before and after holidays out of the calculations. She printed a summary for herself so she could see what the results looked like (see Table 3).

"Now," Lisa thought, "what's next?"

TABLE 3   Teller Cash Transactions.
Average Number of Cash Transactions per Day by Month

Month	1989	1990	1991	1992
January	418.7	454.1	508.4	556.8
February	406.2	462.2	497.8	540.1
March	426.3	462.0	521.2	562.6
April	440.9	482.0	524.6	
May	429.1	471.5	521.8	
June	440.3	489.3	535.6	
July	422.8	474.8	519.1	
August	434.1	475.8	529.6	
September	448.4	507.5	555.5	
October	452.7	489.0	529.6	
November	462.1	511.6	564.0	
December	472.3	510.3	566.5	
Average	438.0	481.8	530.0	

Cash Transactions by Day of the Week

Year	Mon	Tues	Wed	Thur	Fri	Sat
1989	788.1	315.6	329.3	365.0	581.3	247.6
1990	855.4	354.5	341.5	378.4	664.9	300.4
1991	922.4	411.1	363.4	477.2	722.4	290.5
1992	986.4	421.0	405.6	483.7	740.9	336.6

Cash Transactions by Date of the Month

Date	1989	1990	1991	1992
1	458.6	516.5	567.7	596.7
2	463.9	514.6	552.8	581.5
3	458.2	507.4	565.5	619.7
4	475.3	537.2	585.6	602.8
5	481.4	533.4	604.2	609.6
6	452.9	498.7	523.3	622.0
7	447.2	483.3	520.3	556.7
8	417.4	440.9	501.9	519.6
9	405.6	453.4	506.2	505.6

(continued)

TABLE 3   (continued)   Cash Transactions by Date of the Month

Date	1989	1990	1991	1992
10	385.9	465.5	566.1	511.2
11	397.7	430.8	497.7	521.3
12	401.2	449.1	520.5	533.7
13	426.2	465.9	507.0	543.2
14	443.7	497.3	539.7	570.8
15	463.4	514.1	577.2	593.3
16	456.9	484.7	499.2	575.3
17	425.3	455.8	506.2	549.4
18	413.5	439.0	498.7	515.1
19	405.2	439.9	471.2	514.0
20	412.6	434.6	501.9	490.4
21	396.4	435.6	496.1	513.4
22	410.0	461.1	513.4	551.7
23	458.2	532.4	555.4	560.7
24	451.6	508.3	517.8	574.7
25	473.5	500.1	474.5	585.4
26	452.9	489.5	543.4	552.8
27	417.9	456.3	521.0	515.7
28	412.2	461.6	499.8	553.9
29	434.1	492.4	551.8	681.0
30	476.6	504.0	557.1	597.8
31	503.7	534.4	589.4	612.4

CASE 2

NorthCoast Bank: Linear Programming, Integer Programming, and Scheduling

Located in the Great Northern Mall in North Olmsted, Ohio, the North-Coast Bank of Great Northern is one of 40 banks owned and operated by the NorthCoast Bank Holding Company of Ohio. The bank is relatively small, having assets of approximately $35 million, but it has been experiencing a steady growth of about 10% per year. During her first week working as a student intern at NorthCoast-Great Northern, Lisa Stanley was given an assignment to forecast future demand and capacity requirements for tellers. John Homenko, Vice President of Operations, was so pleased with the job she did on that assignment that he asked her to take it a step further and develop some alternative staffing plans and work schedules for the tellers. They agreed that Lisa should take a couple of days to gather some information and think about the problem, and that then the two of them would sit down with Edith Hodge, the head teller, and talk some more about just what direction Lisa would go with the project.

   Lisa talked with Edith and learned about the current situation regarding teller scheduling. The bank's five full-time tellers are scheduled to work 40 hours each week. Their 40 hours are made up of four 9-hour days and one 4-hour day (usually Saturday). They start at 8:30 AM, end at 6:30 PM, and take an unpaid hour for lunch. The teller windows are open from 9:00 AM to 6:00 PM (9:00 AM to noon on Saturday). The schedule allows each teller 1/2 hour to set up for the day and 1/2 hour to close out at the end of his or her shift. Consequently each full-time teller is available for 8 hours of "open-window" time. Edith, who does the scheduling, told Lisa that she tries to send half the tellers to lunch from

12:00 to 1:00 and the other half from 1:00 to 2:00. This isn't carved in stone, but she likes to have as many full-time tellers as possible present at the busy times because of their greater experience, their higher productivity, and their calm under fire.

In addition to the five full-time tellers, the bank has several part-time tellers who are scheduled as needed during the week. By policy, part-time employees are guaranteed a minimum of 3 hours each day they work, and they are not scheduled to work more than 5 hours in a day. Sometimes one or more of the part-time tellers are asked to work longer than their scheduled shift in order to help out with unexpectedly heavy customer traffic. Less frequently, one of the full-time tellers will be asked to work on his or her day off. This, of course, results in overtime. Any overtime hours in excess of 40 hours in a week are paid at time-and-a-half. Anyone, full- or part-time, scheduled to work 4 or more hours consecutively is entitled to a 15-minute break after the first 2 hours. By law everyone must be given a meal break after working 5 hours.

If the customer load at the teller windows gets to be more than the available tellers can handle, someone from one of the bank's other departments can open another window. The other areas that most frequently provide temporary help this way are new accounts and customer service. In a real pinch, however, anyone in the bank, up to and including the President Steve Pence, can help out. "Everyone knows how to do teller duty, and everyone is, in effect, 'on call.'" Normally the maximum number of tellers is twelve (since that is the number of teller windows), but under extreme circumstances they will sometimes double up at a window, that is, put two tellers working at one window. This is not desirable because it creates crowded working conditions and reduces the amount of privacy afforded the customer. It is necessary, however, when the waiting line starts to get unacceptably long.

If, on the other hand, the work load is so light that not all the available tellers are needed at open windows, there are other tasks that they can perform. Included in these other tasks are filing signature cards, filing loan documents, helping out with some of the bookkeeping functions, and other back room activities. When planning her daily staffing schedule, Edith can include up to 4 or 5 hours of teller duty by employees from other areas of the bank. In actual practice, she will use fewer hours than that (if the customer load is lighter than expected) or more hours than that (if the load is heavier than expected).

On Saturday the full-time teller staff is augmented with part-time tellers. Some of these part-timers work in other areas of the bank during the week, some of them work as part-time tellers during the week, and some of them work for NorthCoast only on Saturday.

From the analysis that she had done previously for John, Lisa had a projection of the demand and the desired number of tellers hour by hour for each day of the week for the next two weeks (Table 1).

These "desired number of tellers" figures were calculated based on demand forecasts, service time measurements, and arrival rate estimations that Lisa had made as a part of that earlier project. Using a multiserver queuing model and assuming that all customers wait in a single line for the next available teller, she had calculated the number of tellers needed to provide a level of customer service such that no more than 20% of arriving customers would be expected to wait in line. (She had also completed an analysis based on the assumption that commercial and noncommercial customers waited in separate lines to be served by different tellers, but for the present assignment she decided to use the single-line multiserver model as the basis for her analysis.) The "desired number" does not include any allowance for tellers going on break; that is, they represent the desired number of tellers present and actually working an open teller window.

When Lisa, Edith, and John sat down to discuss what exactly they wanted the new schedule to accomplish, John indicated that he wanted to have at least the "desired number" of tellers (as calculated by Lisa) to provide the level of service upon which those numbers were based. He also wanted to have a schedule that the employees would like at least as much as the current schedule. Of course, he wanted to keep the costs as

TABLE 1 Desired Number of Tellers Hour by Hour for Each Day of the Week

Hour of the Day	M	T	W	T	F	S	M	T	W	T	F	S
9–10	6	4	3	4	5	8	6	3	3	3	5	9
10–11	8	4	4	4	6	8	7	4	4	4	6	9
11–12	13(10)	7	6	7	9	8	11	6	6	7	10	9
12–1	15(12)	8	7	8	11		13(10)	7	7	8	12	
1–2	9	5	5	5	6		8	4	4	5	7	
2–3	6	3	3	3	4		5	3	3	3	5	
3–4	4	3	2	3	3		4	2	2	3	3	
4–5	5	3	3	3	4		5	3	3	3	4	
5–6	16(13)	8	8	8	11		14(11)	7	7	8	13(10)	

Notes: Entries are the number of tellers required to provide a level of customer service such that a customer has less than a 20% probability of having to wait for service. Numbers in parentheses are based on a level of service such that customers have less than a 70% probability of waiting for service *and* the expected wait will be less than 3 minutes for *those who actually do wait*.

low as possible. After talking for a while, they decided that Lisa would schedule the desired number of tellers as long as that number didn't exceed twelve. If that number did exceed twelve, she would schedule twelve tellers unless more were required to meet the following customer service level: The percentage of customers having to wait for service shall be less than 70% *and* the expected waiting time *of those who do wait* shall be less than 3 minutes. She would schedule enough tellers to meet this lower standard of customer service, and the tellers would have to double up.

The three of them agreed that personnel costs were the only costs that would be included in the analysis. The wage and benefit costs of employees helping out from other departments would be included so as to get an accurate picture of the true cost of providing teller services. John indicated that the "four-nines-and-a-four" schedule could not be modified, but other factors, such as the timing of the lunch hour, could be modified if there were good reason. He encouraged Lisa to experiment with some "alternative staffing and scheduling" patterns that might use more or fewer full-time tellers than were currently on staff. Edith indicated that she wouldn't object to using more part-time tellers, just as long as there were always as least as many full-timers as part-timers working at any hour of the day.

The personnel office at the NorthCoast Bank Holding Company, which handles personnel matters for all the subsidiary banks, gave Lisa figures for personnel costs (Table 2). Lisa sat down at her desk to think about how she might approach this task and to produce a new schedule for the bank.

TABLE 2   Wage and Benefit Costs for Teller Personnel

Personnel	Average Hourly Cost
Full-time teller	$11.93 per hour for regular-time hours. (This cost includes an average of $9.86 per hour for salary [based on 40 hours weekly] and an average of 21% for benefits.)
	$15.90 for any overtime in excess of 40 hours in a given week. (This cost would apply to any non-teller full-time employee working a teller window after 5:00 PM.)
Part-time teller	$7.61 per hour

CASE 3   NorthCoast Bank: Strategy and Location

The NorthCoast Bank Holding Company of Ohio owns and operates 40 NorthCoast Banks throughout the state of Ohio. NorthCoast Bank, which is known for its conservative lending practices and innovation in customer service, has pursued an aggressive growth strategy since its inception. The first of the banks that were to become NorthCoast Banks was chartered in 1963 as the Westgate National Bank. The bank opened on February 28, 1963, in a temporary office trailer in the Westgate Mall in Rocky River, Ohio. A suburb of Cleveland, Rocky River was projected to be an area of significant population and commercial growth. Westgate National was an immediate success; it attracted $737,000 in 270 accounts on opening day. By the end of May, after only three months of operations, the deposits had increased to $1,261,000 in 807 accounts. By the end of 1964, deposits had grown to more than $3.7 million in nearly 5000 accounts, and the bank made their first profit, $2800.

The bank moved from the trailer to a newly constructed building on the same site in June 1963. By 1970 Westgate National, which later became NorthCoast Bank of Westgate, had outgrown its building, so it began construction of its own seven-story office building on another site within the shopping center. The bank moved into its new offices in January 1972. Today it still occupies the first two floors of that building. The parent company, NorthCoast Bank Holding Company of Ohio, is housed on the upper floors and the middle floors are rented out.

The early success led the directors of the Westgate National Bank to seek to expand. The first attempt at expansion was an application, filed in August 1964, for a charter to open an affiliate bank in the Great

Northern Mall. This application was denied in the summer of 1965. Subsequently the bank shareholders bought the Solon Bank (Solon, Ohio) with the intention of converting it from a state charter to a national charter and moving it to Great Northern. When the National Bank Supervisors indicated a reluctance to approve this move, the strategy was changed and approval was sought and received from the State Banking Board for the move. Unfortunately the State Banking Board delayed in issuing its narrowly worded decision approving the move of Solon to become the "only" commercial bank *in* the Great Northern Mall.

Shortly before the State Banking Board issued its approval, the financially troubled 9th Street National Bank received permission from the Comptroller of the Currency to move from downtown Cleveland to the Great Northern Mall. Since only one bank was to be allowed in Great Northern and since the approval to move Solon required that it be located *in* the shopping center, not *near* it, the move never happened. Although the failure to move into Great Northern was a disappointment, the purchase of the Solon Bank turned out to be a profitable move. It is still operating today as NorthCoast Bank of Solon. It wasn't until 1981 that the goal of having a Great Northern bank was realized, when NorthCoast Bank of Great Northern opened on land adjacent to the mall.

Attention was turned to Chagrin Falls, Ohio. A state charter was issued in late 1967 to open a bank in Chagrin Falls. As part of the establishment of the Bank of Chagrin Falls (now NorthCoast Bank of Chagrin Falls), WNB, Inc., a new subsidiary to the original holding company, was formed. WNB became the holding company for the Berea National Bank, which was chartered and opened in 1969. Through a series of strategic maneuvers between 1970 and 1972, WNB became the parent holding company for all the banks then owned by Westgate. During the period while the restructuring was taking place, two more banks, the Sandusky Bank (now NorthCoast Bank of Sandusky) and the Parma National Bank (now NorthCoast Bank of Parma), were opened. When the restructuring was completed in June 1972, WNB changed its name to Westgate Banks, Inc.

During the next ten years, eleven more banks opened, including the NorthCoast Bank of Great Northern. The name Westgate Banks was changed to NorthCoast Bank Holding Company in early 1978, and all the banks were renamed "NorthCoast Bank of ... ." In 1980, in another strategic maneuver, NorthCoast Bank Holding Company was restructured to become NorthCoast Bank Holding Company of Ohio. In 1987 NorthCoast Bank adopted a strategy of opening banks in grocery stores. Agreement was reached with Jordan's SuperMarkets (which operates more than 100 grocery stores in Ohio) and ten National Charter Applications were submitted in November 1987. All applications were approved, and ten banks were opened in Jordan's SuperMarkets around the Greater Cleveland area.

The NorthCoast Bank of Great Northern (or simply Great Northern) is near the intersection of two main thoroughfares, Lorain Road and Brookpark Road. It occupies the entire first floor of a five-story building on land adjacent to the Great Northern Mall, which is one of the largest shopping malls in Cleveland. Although it is not, technically, a part of Great Northern, the bank sits right next to the mall and fronts along Lorain Road. The entrance to the bank's parking area is off one of the main roadways leading to the mall.

Steve Pence, President of NorthCoast Bank of Great Northern, has been working with Susan Schultz and Ed James from the Holding Company to analyze the possibility of opening a new bank in the unincorporated area just to the southwest of North Olmsted. The decision is actually several decisions in one. Should NorthCoast Bank open any bank in this area? If yes, how soon should it be opened? Where should it be located? In what type of facility should the bank be located? How big should it be? What products and services should be included or not included?

Steve asked Lisa Stanley, a student intern from a nearby university, to help him and the others analyze the location decision. Lisa, who is majoring in Operations Management, had already completed two projects for John Homenko, the Vice President of Operations. She was eager to tackle this new assignment. She talked with Steve about the decision.

In the words of Steve Pence:

> The decision of whether a bank should or should not be opened in this area hinges almost entirely on the question of profitability potential. All our demographic and economic projections indicate that this area will be able to support two, or maybe three, banks profitably. We are better suited to the type of demand that will develop there than most of our competitors.

> The question of timing depends on the growth and development of the area and on our ability to devote resources and energy to this project given other activities and opportunities underway now and in the near future. It also depends on what the competition is doing, or is likely to do in the near future.

> The location decision and the type of facility question are closely related. The team reviewing the situation has identified three promising alternative sites. NorthCoast has an option on a plot of land located at the intersection of two roads that already carry substantial traffic. The

area immediately around this intersection is expected to see heavy commercial development, with residential neighborhoods surrounding the commercial center. The two roads will be the main arteries carrying traffic into, out of, and through the area. If the land is purchased, two options are under consideration. One option is to erect a bank-only building which would house the bank, with room for anticipated expansion. The extra space not immediately needed for bank operations would be rented out until anticipated growth made it necessary to convert it to bank use. The second option is to build a multistory office building with the bank occupying the ground floor and renting the remainder of the space.

The second potential site is an already existing strip mall on one of the roads mentioned above, about one mile east from the intersection mentioned above. There are two options at this site. A Jordan's SuperMarket grocery situated at one end of the strip could house a NorthCoast Bank similar to those in other Jordan's SuperMarkets. The second option would entail opening a mini-bank in a store front in the center of the strip. This bank would be similar in size and operation to the mini-banks in the Jordan's SuperMarket, but it would afford somewhat more flexibility in operations than the Jordan's SuperMarket site.

The third potential site is about a mile south of the first site. A new shopping center is going to be built near the expressway that runs around the south side of Cleveland. Since the shopping center is not yet fully developed, NorthCoast Bank would have several options. Two options involve negotiating with the developer to buy a section of land and building its own stand-alone building (either a bank-only or a multistory office building). Another option is locating in a Jordan's SuperMarket that will stand separate from the mall but will share a section of the parking lot with it. A fourth option is renting space in the mall, space that would permit entrance to the bank from either inside the mall or from outside. A fifth option is to negotiate with the developer to build a stand-alone bank and rent it to NorthCoast Bank.

After her talk with Steve, Lisa arranged to meet with Ed James. Ed discussed the three potential locations and the different types of facilities that might be established.

The location depends, I think, on the growth projections. We have estimated the probability of several growth scenarios. Both population growth and commercial development are important. Of course, they are related to one another. For purposes of simplifying the problem, the possible scenarios of population and commercial growth each were broken down into three possibilities: high, medium, and low growth. We believe that the probabilities of the different levels of commercial growth are somewhat dependent on the population growth rate. Steve,

Susan, and I each estimated the probabilities of the different growth rates. We also got similar estimates from several other people in the bank and from outside the bank.

Then we combined the individual estimates to get a composite estimate that there is a 50% chance of high population growth, a 30% chance of medium growth, and a 20% chance of low growth. The combined estimates of the commercial growth rate varied, depending on the assumed population growth rate. If the population growth is high, the estimated probabilities for high, medium, and low commercial growth are 80%, 20%, and 0%, respectively. If the population growth is medium, the estimated probabilities for high, medium, and low commercial growth are 60%, 30%, and 10%, respectively. If the population growth is low, the estimated probabilities for high, medium, and low commercial growth are 40%, 40%, and 20%, respectively.

Although the population growth will take place throughout the area, we have plotted out seven centers of growth and projected the populations for each of the centers under each of the assumed growth rates.

Ed gave Lisa a schematic map of the area. The map had the three potential locations and the seven population centers marked on it. Accompanying the map was a table with values for the high, medium, and low population growth scenarios (Table 1 and Figure 1).
Ed discussed additional considerations related to the decision.

There are more than 1500 banks inside grocery stores around the country. It's a very successful concept. It costs only $200,000 to $400,000 to put a 300- to 600-square-foot mini-bank in a grocery store; compare this to $1 million or more to build a new bank building. Further, an

TABLE 1   Population Projections

Population Center	Current Population	Population Assuming Growth Rate is		
		High	Medium	Low
A	2,312	24,276	8,554	5,318
B	1,187	17,330	8,546	2,137
C	756	4,158	3,553	2,948
D	1,355	9,214	7,046	3,252
E	212	5,915	4,558	996
F	33	3,564	2,574	132
G	0	11,500	8,000	0
Total	5,855	75,957	42,831	14,783

Figure 1 **NorthCoast Bank Expansion Opportunities**

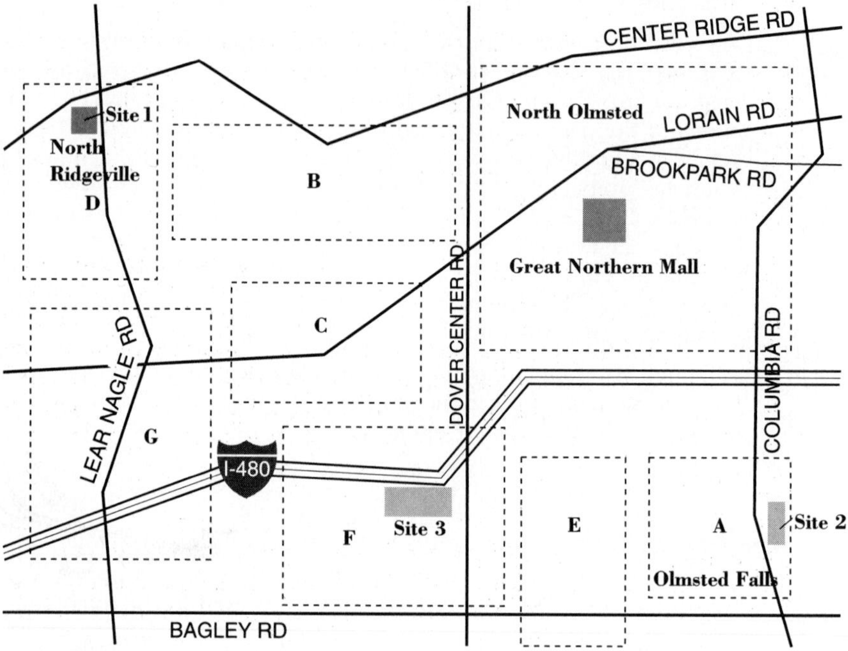

in-store bank can be opened in as little as 90 days, whereas it takes a year or more to build a new free-standing bank. We have been very successful with the banks we have put in Jordan's SuperMarkets. We have picked up $47,000,000 in 37,000 new accounts and more than 25,000 new customers since we began putting in the grocery banks. Banking has changed a lot in the last 15 years. It used to be that a banker was this conservative guy who sat behind a desk waiting for the customer to come to him. Now we've become like a retail business. We are still conservative in our loan practices, but we are going out to where the customer is instead of making him or her come to us. We talk about product. Marketing, sales, and customer service are important parts of our business.

If we put a bank in Jordan's SuperMarket, we have immediate exposure to 15,000 to 25,000 people per week, sometimes more. These aren't just people, they're potential customers. If 20% of them are our customers, that's 3000 customers, many of them new to NorthCoast. Equally valuable is the fact that the other 80% are customers of our competitors. Where else can you get daily contact and a chance to sell to your competitors' customers?

After talking with Ed, Lisa talked with Susan Schultz. Susan is the Senior Vice President of Planning. An economist by training, she represents another major trend in the banking business, the advance of women into the upper ranks of management. Nearly one-third of North-Coast's officers and managers are women. Susan had done most of the economic research for the new bank.

Yes, there is a tremendous push toward making banking more convenient. The only thing more convenient than in-store banking is at-home banking. We will be a leader in that area, but that won't really take off for a few years yet, and then there will still be a need and a market for in-store banks and stand-alone neighborhood banks. The in-store banks are great for bringing in new depositors, but they are not nearly as good a source of new loans. Not many of the new accounts are commercial, and people tend to view the in-store banks as not much more than check-cashing centers. We will have to do a lot more marketing if we are going to sell the idea that the in-store locations are real banks. We offer a pretty full range of products, but we don't, for example, offer safety deposit boxes and we don't have a vault. For security reasons we don't keep a lot of cash on hand at the in-store banks. Each of the in-store banks is affiliated with a regular bank that services them.

We haven't tried a store-front bank in a mall. That's something we are looking at. It would certainly locate us where there are lots of people. But frankly, in my opinion, in-mall stores do not offer quite as much convenience as grocery banks. Although both get you exposure to a lot of people, they provide a different type of image and visibility than the traditional free-standing bank. In the minds of a lot of people, there's something reassuring and impressive about a bank building. It creates more of a presence; it represents more of a commitment to the community. It becomes a landmark; people give directions by saying "We're right across the street from the NorthCoast Bank."

The in-store banks are particularly useful for establishing beachheads or as backfill. They can get us into a new community quickly and inexpensively, or they can fill in the gaps between our free-standing banks. We have to be careful that the profile of the store and its customers matches our profile. This will be one key to whether or not a particular in-store bank will be successful.

We have projected the total assets and the return on assets for each facility option at each location option (see Table 2). All options project out to be profitable if the growth is there. If both the population and

TABLE 2 Total Assets & Return on Assets (%) Three Years After Opening

Population Growth	High			Medium			Low		
Commercial Growth	High	Medium	Low	High	Medium	Low	High	Medium	Low
Site 1									
Free Standing									
Assets	11,211	9,837	7,782	9,571	8,693	6,457	5,217	4,377	2,613
ROA (%)	2.08	1.96	1.32	1.92	1.81	1.21	1.64	1.38	0.78
Office Bldg									
Assets	15,036	13,614	11,448	13,373	12,444	10,001	8,939	8,074	6,224
ROA (%)	2.17	1.91	1.05	2.04	1.77	0.98	1.81	1.17	0.52
Site 2									
Grocery Bank									
Assets	9,801	8,577	6,691	8,150	7,345	5,218	3,893	3,062	1,568
ROA (%)	2.24	2.11	1.86	2.02	1.90	1.71	1.71	1.44	0.84
Mall Store Front									
Assets	9,772	8,523	6,623	8,097	7,288	5,155	3,821	3,007	1,546
ROA (%)	2.21	2.08	1.82	1.97	1.86	1.66	1.68	1.41	0.81
Site 3									
Free Standing									
Assets	11,343	9,948	7,884	9,636	8,710	6,425	5,200	4,309	2,510
ROA (%)	2.18	2.07	1.48	2.01	1.89	1.25	1.68	1.42	0.82
Office Bldg									
Assets	15,248	13,752	11,522	13,460	12,467	9,956	8,982	8,042	6,092
ROA (%)	2.22	2.01	1.06	2.11	1.81	1.03	1.93	1.22	0.56
Grocery Bank									
Assets	9,896	8,654	6,752	8,201	7,348	5,174	3,871	3,007	1,505
ROA (%)	2.27	2.14	1.91	2.05	1.93	1.75	1.74	1.47	0.88
Mall Store Front									
Assets	9,865	8,596	6,679	8,143	7,285	5,107	3,795	2,946	1,478
ROA (%)	2.24	2.11	1.84	2.02	1.89	1.70	1.71	1.45	0.86

commercial growth rates are either medium or high, the projected ROAs (Return on Assets) are all in the range of 1.8% to 2.2% after the first couple of years. The grocery banks are less expensive, quicker, and easier to set up. They become profitable a year or two sooner than free-standing banks. Like I said, we haven't used store-front banks in malls before, but we project that they will be similar in cost, operation, and profitability to the grocery banks.

The projected ROAs for the grocery and store-front options are slightly higher than that for the free-standing bank options. This is primarily due to their lower initial costs and lower operating costs. Their deposit base would be somewhat smaller than a free-standing bank, and the number and size of loans will be less, but with the lower cost the ROA is slightly better.

Long term, the potential at the new mall out by the expressway offers slightly better returns for each type of facility compared to the same type of facility at either of the other locations. On the other hand, it will take nearly two years longer to get a bank open out there compared to the other locations.

Besides profitability, we need to consider several other factors. For example, how would each of the options fit with our current strategy? (What, for that matter, should our strategy be?) What impact will each option have on our visibility and image in the community? What is the competition doing? Social responsibility has become something we talk about a lot more lately. What does a particular option contribute to the community? How does it add to or detract from our desire to be socially responsible?

When Lisa pressed Susan on the matter of the various "other factors," Susan was able to venture an educated guess that profitability and strategic fit are the two most important factors, with profitability being "half-again as important as strategic fit." She thought that strategic fit "is about three times as important as what our competitors are doing" which, in turn, is "about the same level of importance as our visibility in the community." The fifth factor mentioned by Susan is social responsibility, which she judged to be "only half as important as either visibility or competitors' actions." Finally, Susan acknowledged that no one had rated the various locations and/or options on these criteria, but that it might be a good idea if someone did so.

COMPANY 4

PDQ PRINTING

CASE 1   PDQ Printing: Strategy and Location

Jon Dominick, the owner of PDQ Printing in Evergreen, Colorado, set down the year-end financial statements. "1986 was a good year," he thought as he sat back in his chair. "Sales and profits are both up, not as much as I would like, but the growth is continuing." Jon had purchased the business in August 1979 and total revenues that year had been only $80,000. This year closed with PDQ generating about $580,000 in gross revenue. This was an increase of $42,000 from the preceding year. In general, the business is quite profitable with an average after-tax profit of almost 6%.

PDQ Printing is a moderate-sized, general-purpose printer. The typical customer is a small business or individual needing letterhead, business cards, newsletters, flyers, membership rosters, or similar types of printing. The average job length this past year has been about 1000 pieces. They do some two-color printing, but almost no three- or four-color work. The shop has two AB Dick 375 presses, but both are one-color presses. PDQ can do simple binding, but any perfect binding must be sent out to a subcontractor. They can do some basic typesetting and graphics, but much of this is also subcontracted. Customers typically expect their orders to be completed in three to seven days and often are quite flexible. However, Jon knows he must be done by the promised completion date or the customers will be unhappy. About three-quarters of the orders are picked up at the shop. The rest are delivered. Last year Jon started regular pick up and delivery service for his Denver customers, and that segment of the business is growing quickly. Of course, some of his customers like the 35-mile drive up into the mountains and

101

deliver and pick up their work. The scenery is terrific and the quality of life is superb. That is, after all, why Jon and his wife decided to move to Evergreen from Denver.

When Jon redecorated the customer service area two years ago, he put his office at the north end. Except for the wood door that is generally open anyway, the entire wall separating him from the customers and front counter people is glass. He can see all the customers who enter the shop. This allows him the opportunity to greet his regular customers personally and easily establish a relationship with new customers. It also allows him to be readily available to help solve customer problems. He prides himself on the personal relationships he has developed with many of his customers over the years and feels this personal touch helps separate PDQ from other printers in the area.

Jon believes that the success of PDQ is strongly linked to the quality and timeliness of their work. Making sure the customer receives his order on time has been challenging as the business has continued to grow, but in general they do a good job. The quality issue has also been a challenge. The two AB Dick 375 presses in the shop are old and need constant attention to ensure high-quality output. They are in need of rebuilding or replacement. Of course, rebuilding is much cheaper and does restore the press to almost new condition. It is difficult to do two-color printing on these presses because it requires two completely different setups, one for each color. The biggest challenge is making sure the registration is acceptable. Registration is the alignment of each color image on the sheet of paper. On presses equipped to do two-color printing it is much easier to maintain good registration. Either or both of the 375s could be equipped to do two-color printing during a rebuild for very little extra cost.

The general-purpose segment of the printing business has been growing strongly for the past decade and all the projections that Jon has seen indicate it will continue to do so for the next several years. Jon is very interested in continuing to expand the business. In March 1983 he purchased a small print shop in Aspen Park. Aspen Park is a small town of under 5000 people located about 10 miles south of Evergreen (see Figure 1). This shop has an old and relatively slow one-color AB Dick automated system that prints and binds in one operation. The Aspen Park location does about the same type of business as the main shop in Evergreen, but it is considerably more rural. Although this looked like a good deal at the time he bought it, the Aspen Park location has yet to be profitable. In 1986 Aspen Park contributed a net loss of $5,000. This brought the total loss from the Aspen Park location to $16,000.

Figure 1 *Denver Area Layout*

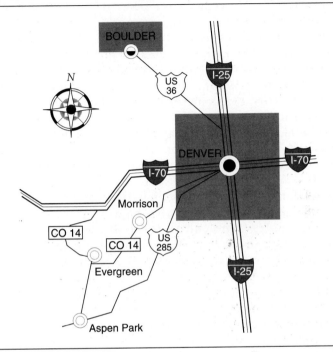

Jon has noticed that customers seem to be placing bigger and bigger orders. The average job size has grown about 15% in the past three years. Further, more customers are requesting two-color printing, and some of his better customers are bringing in small books and journals to be printed. The change has been slow, but Jon is beginning to wonder. "Is this the start of a trend?" he thought as he looked at the jobs waiting to be picked up. "If my customers want more sophisticated printing, I need to be thinking about acquiring new capabilities."

Just two days earlier, Jon had been over at Winter Park Printing, a small commercial printer a few miles away in Morrison. Sam Boyd is the owner of Winter Park Printing, and he told Jon he was ready to retire. He has been running the business for 32 years and thought it was time to relax. His sons don't seem very interested in picking up the business, so Sam asked Jon if he knew anyone who might be interested in buying Winter Park Printing.

Commercial printing is a completely different segment of the printing business. Jobs are typically 10,000 to 50,000 pieces and many are two or more colors. This is the segment of the business that prints books, magazines, catalogs, calendars, and other high-volume products. Customers typically book orders weeks or months in advance with rigidly specified due dates, though there is the occasional rush order. Camera-ready originals are shipped to the printer, and the completed work is shipped back to the customer. The basic printing technology is the same, but the actual presses are dramatically different. The small presses at PDQ use individual sheets of paper and can print about 5000 impressions per hour. The big commercial presses often use rolls of paper and can print as many as 20,000 equivalent impressions in an hour. Further, they all print two sides at once and some can easily handle four-color jobs. Winter Park Printing has three commercial presses with slightly different capabilities. One is a very-high-capacity four-color press, and two are slightly slower two-color presses. Jon has been using Winter Park as a subcontractor for the occasional large jobs that his customers bring to PDQ. He doesn't want to refuse the big jobs, even though he re-

TABLE 1   Winter Park Printing Financial Summary – 1985

Income		
Sales		$1,457,000
Other		$7,000
Expenses		
Supplies	$299,000	
Advertising	22,000	
Transportation	165,000	
Insurance	150,000	
Wages & Salaries	542,000	
Equipment Depreciation	4,000	
Maintenance	86,000	
Rent	91,000	
Telephone	10,000	
Utilities	12,000	
Other	20,000	
Total	$1,401,000	$1,464,000
Profit (Loss)	$63,000	

TABLE 2   Winter Park Printing Booked Orders – Oct/Dec 1986

Customer	Revenue	Due Date
Mountain Life	$28,000	10/1
Winter Park Business Assoc.	$6,000	10/6
Mountain Life	$28,000	10/15
Columbine Home	$10,000	10/18
High Plains Books	$15,000	10/22
South Denver Reader	$8,000	10/24
Fred Jones Appliances	$12,000	10/25
Denver Times	$8,000	10/12
Denver Times	$10,000	10/26
Mountain Life	$28,000	11/1
Vail Hotel Assoc.	$8,000	11/4
Black Canyon Press	$17,000	11/4
High Plains Books	$11,000	11/20
Mountain Life	$28,000	11/15
Evergreen Home Buyers Guide	$5,000	11/25
Denver Apartment Shoppers	$7,000	11/26
Denver Times	$19,000	11/10
Mountain Life	$28,000	12/1

ally can't do them, because the customer may then take the small jobs elsewhere.

"This might be just what I need," Jon thought. "If I bought Winter Park, I could get the high-volume capability I need and expand into new markets, grow the business! Let's see, Sam gave me some recent financials (see Table 1) and a list of the booked orders for the next three months (see Table 2). I should look these over. He also said he would carry the note on the business because he knew the profit would more than cover the financing."

CASE 2 PDQ Printing: Layout, Scheduling, and Process Design

"Boy, there is nothing quite like owning your own business," Jon Dominick thought as he set down the phone. "It's just like a prize fight. As soon as you sit down, the bell rings and you're up at it again." One of his regular customers, the local APICS Chapter, had just called with a serious complaint. The APICS Chapter prints nine 8- to 10-page newsletters, a membership roster, and several seminar announcements each year and is considered a valued customer. Their November newsletter was printed and delivered very late. Since the newsletter is their primary vehicle for informing the Chapter of monthly meetings, this late printing and delivery contributed to a very sparse turnout for the November meeting. Jon was very unhappy about this and did some investigating. The invoice (which was completed when the order was placed) didn't have a due date on it. This is a critical piece of information for the shop.

Scheduling the jobs to be run is a fairly intuitive process at PDQ Printing. When an order is received, the front counter people immediately load it into the first day that seems to have time available, typically three to five days in the future. This varies somewhat, depending on the type of work, the length of time it will take to print, special paper or ink requirements, and other relevant issues. For example, typesetting may take several days for a complex document, and the customer needs to review it before printing. Typeset jobs are not loaded into the schedule for printing until after the typesetting and customer review. The average day has about 40 jobs scheduled to be run.

In any case, if the customer requests a due date earlier than the first available day, the front counter people try to accommodate. They will place the order in with the work already allocated for an earlier day. If this seems to make the workload excessive on that day, one or more of the jobs already loaded may be pulled and moved to a later day. A considerable amount of "cascading" can result when this happens. Fortunately this doesn't happen very often. The front counter people try to leave a little extra capacity in each day just to absorb these rush jobs. Each day is generally completely full by the afternoon before. When orders must be moved, the people at the front counter usually, but not always, check with the shop so these changes and additions are not a complete surprise. In his investigation, Jon discovered the APICS newsletter was moved to a slot several days later than its original loading because of a "cascade" of replanning.

Gary Smith, the Production Manager, does the detail scheduling for each day. Before he goes home each night, Gary pulls all the work orders for the next day. He wants to know what is scheduled so he can best sequence the jobs. Table 1 is a typical assortment of work orders for one day. Gary has developed an informal system that considers the amount of work on each press, press capacities, ink colors (lightest first), due date and time, and other requirements. If there is not enough work in the current day's jobs to keep his presses busy, he may pull some work from the next day or two to fill the capacity. Of course, any job left over from the current day's work needs to go into the work for the next day. Occasionally an unrealistic amount of work is loaded into a particular day, and Gary has to decide which jobs will be moved to subsequent days. The APICS newsletter, which was scheduled for late completion because of the missing due date and the "cascade" of rescheduling, was rescheduled even later when press problems caused some jobs to run longer than expected. The missing due date let Gary reschedule it several days later in the job stream. By now, even though the original loading would have resulted in an on-time completion, the job was actually completed eight days late.

There have been several problems like the APICS newsletter recently. Not all of them have been related to scheduling. One job was printed on the wrong paper, they failed to include the typesetting charges on one invoice, and one job should have been delivered to a mailing service but was held for the customer by mistake. Jon believes these problems are due to three separate causes. One cause is incomplete or incorrect invoices. If the due date, type of paper stock, or delivery instructions are not on the invoice or are not correct, the shop has no basis on which to schedule the job, print it properly, or deliver it to the

TABLE 1 Work Orders for November 14

WO#	Copies	Estimated Finish Time (hrs)	Ink Color	Due Date	Comments
3624	1250	3.00	Lt Green	11/18	Trim, Collate, Bind
3625	500	0.25	Red	11/14	
	250	0.25	Black	11/14	
3626	2000	1.00	Black	11/16	Glossy, Collate
3627	750	0.50	Green	11/14	Trim
3628	1000	0.25	Brown	11/15	
3629	2500	0.50	Yellow	11/20	Trim
3630	500	1.25	Black	11/14	Trim, Collate, Staple
3631	500	0.75	Black	11/16	Trim, Collate
3632	1250	2.00	Black	11/17	Glossy, Trim, Collate, Bind
3633	750	0.25	Dk Green	11/15	
3634	1500	1.00	Black	11/15	Collate, Perfect Bind
	100	0.25	Dk Blue	11/15	
	250	0.25	Lt Brown	11/14	
3635	2400	1.00	Maroon	11/14	Collate
3636	1250	0.25	Black/Green	11/15	
3637	500	1.00	Black	11/17	Trim, Collate
3638	750	1.50	Red	11/15	Trim, Collate
3639	1000	0.25	Black	11/16	Glossy
3640	1750	0.25	Black	11/14	
3641	600	0.50	Black/Red	11/19	Trim
3642	1200	1.00	Black	11/14	Trim, Collate
3643	900	0.75	Black	11/15	
3644	1750	2.25	Green/Black	11/15	Trim, Collate, Bind
3645	1400	0.25	Black	11/14	

(continued)

TABLE 1 (continued)

WO#	Copies	Estimated Finish Time (hrs)	Ink Color	Due Date	Comments
3647	250	0.25	Red/Green	11/14	Glossy
3648	750	0.50	Dk Blue	11/14	Trim
3649	100	0.25	Lt Green	11/14	Glossy
3650	500	2.00	Black	11/14	Trim, Collate, Bind
3651	1100	1.00	Dk Green/Red	11/16	Collate
3652	1600	0.50	Brown	11/16	
3653	500	0.25	Red	11/14	
3654	1150	0.75	Green	11/14	Trim
3655	1600	0.25	Lt Blue	11/15	
3656	900	1.75	Dk Blue	11/17	Trim, Collate, Bind
3657	1200	0.25	Black/Lt Blue	11/18	Glossy
3658	800	0.50	Black/Lt Blue	11/22	Trim
3659	1750	0.25	Black	11/15	

Notes:
- WOs 3625 and 3634 require two different paper stocks.
- WOs 3637, 3642, 3645, 3547, 3651, 3657, and 3658 are two-color jobs.
- WOs 3624, 3632, 3645, 3650, and 3656 can be bound in house.
- Comments describe work above and beyond normal finish activities.
- Each press is scheduled to run 8 hours each day without overtime. This includes all setup and clean up time. Maximum overtime is limited to 2 hours/day/person.
- Each job requires a basic setup time of 0.25 hours. This includes cleaning the press, adjusting it for the appropriate paper size, making the plate, and fixing it in place. Extra clean up and plate times must be considered if required.
- Clean up after a two-color run is an additional 0.15 hours longer, and this must be added to the setup time for the next job to be run on the press.
- Each AB Dick 375 press can print about 4950 copies per hour, not including setup, cleaning, plate making, or other maintenance activities. The AB Dick automated press can print only about 725 copies per hour, not including setup, cleaning, plate making, or other maintenance activities.
- Estimated Finish Time is the estimated time to trim, collate, bind, package, and perform all other finishing work. This includes completing the shop paperwork. Minimum Estimated Finish Time is 0.25 hours.

correct destination. There is really no excuse for the front counter personnel failing to put this information on the invoice accurately. No new people have been hired recently, so all the employees should be very familiar with the requirements.

The second cause is more complicated. The current system calls for a multipart invoice to be completed when the work is brought into the shop (Figure 1). This invoice contains the job specifics and cost estimates. The top two copies (white and yellow) are typically held at the front counter for reference. If there is typesetting work, the yellow copy acts as the work order for the typesetter. It accompanies the order while the typesetting is being done, and the typesetter records her actual charges on this copy. When the typesetting is complete, the camera-ready copy and the work order are returned to the front counter. The printing cannot be scheduled until the typesetting is proofed and approved by the customer. The third (pink) copy circulates with the job in the shop. The form was designed so that only part of the information is transferred through to the yellow and pink copies. The estimated time and cost information shows only on the white copy. That area on the yellow and pink copies is used to record the actual job time and cost information when the work is done. The front counter personnel then manually transfer the cost data to the white copy. To completely reconstruct the details of the order, it is necessary to review the information on all three copies.

When the job is complete, the cost information on the white copy is used for invoicing the customer. If the information is not properly transferred back to the white copy, the billing is inaccurate and the shop may lose money! That error has happened several times over the past few months, and Jon, understandably, is not very happy about it. Although it wouldn't have solved the problem with the APICS newsletter, Jon wonders if a redesign of the entire invoice/shop order process might be beneficial. It might solve some of the other problems as well.

Jon believes the third cause of the recent problems is that the shop is essentially running at full capacity. In the past, the strain of such an effort has led to mistakes. He is planning to add a new press to increase the capacity. This should eliminate some of the problems, but he does need to fit the new press into the existing shop. It is going to require moving some of the equipment to new locations. Will a new layout, Jon wonders, ease some of the problems?

The shop has grown in a somewhat haphazard fashion since Jon bought it 12 years ago. He has expanded and remodeled the building and added equipment as needed, but without any master plan. He currently has three printing presses, a paper cutter, a folder, a collator, a

Figure 1 PDQ Printing Sample Invoice

pdq PRINTING

dominic publications, Inc.
p.o. box 849, evergreen, co 80439
(303) 674-0174
fax (303) 674-2860

date: _____   4506
sold to: _____
attn: _____
phone: _____

proof date _____
print date _____
delivery date _____
date called/proof _____
date called/proof _____
date called/ready _____

qty	imp/side	description	print size	finished size	paper color	paper type	wt	#	sides	units	amount

☐ explanation

☐ black ink   ink _____
                     ink _____
see ☐ neg   ☐ plate
    ☐ art file
☐ typeset units

Instructions:

☐ typesetting/art

☐ camera dept.   ☐ paste-up units

☐ pressroom

☐ shipping   ☐ return art
                     ☐ paper ordered

☐ drill
☐ number #
☐ staple
☐ collate
☐ pad
☐ cut
☐ fold
☐ ink change
☐ graphics
☐ pmt
☐ plate
☐ negatives
☐ h/f 85 line 133 line

sub total _____
shipping charges _____
sub total _____
sales tax _____
total _____

THIS IS YOUR INVOICE!

graphics and camera work is always an estimate

I hereby state that I am authorized to sign this invoice for credit on behalf of the above business or individual and that the above name or business is responsible for payment of any debts incurred. I further state that all goods received on this invoice are to my satisfaction. If litigation is necessary I agree to pay all legal fees and court costs.

received by: _____

Figure 2 PDQ Printing Shop Floor Layout

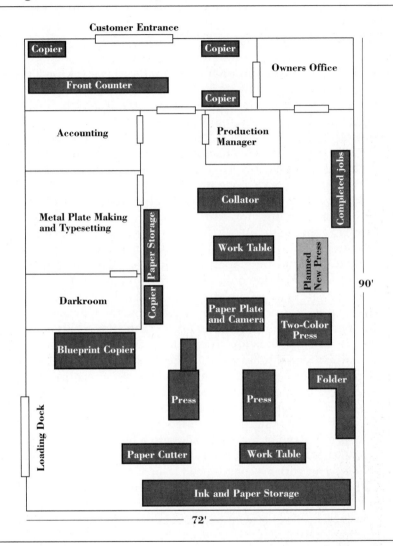

paper plate camera, a large format copier, and a blueprint copier on the shop floor (Figure 2). He is definitely going to add a new printing press and will probably replace his current collator with one that collates and folds in one operation. The large format copier could be moved up front, but it is complicated and expensive to operate. Keeping it in the shop

113

helps control its use. The blueprint copier is a very complex piece of machinery and, even though they do not use it very often, it has no substitute. The building they occupy was originally a movie theater. The floor has been built up to be level and some interior walls have been added. However, none of the interior walls are load bearing, and the entire space is free of columns or other supports. This gives Jon a great deal of flexibility in equipment location.

Although there are many differences between jobs, once orders are taken, they all follow roughly the same set of steps through the shop. The operator of the press selected to run the job prepares the press for the size stock and color ink. This setup starts with cleaning the press from the previous job. This is why Gary tries to schedule light inks first—it makes the cleaning process easier and shorter. If a lighter ink is run after a dark ink, an additional twelve minutes must be added to the setup time for the more difficult cleaning. Additionally PDQ uses mostly rubber-based inks, which can remain in the machine exposed to the air for at least 24 hours without drying. However, they do take longer to dry on the paper, and thus they cannot be used on glossy paper. Any jobs printed on glossy paper require oil-based inks. Changing a press between rubber- and oil-based inks takes an additional twelve minutes each time the change is made. However, normal clean up after oil-based inks takes no longer than after rubber-based inks if no ink base change is made. The plates are prepared, fixed in place, and paper is loaded into the press. If the job requires a metal plate, an additional ten minutes of setup time is necessary. This doesn't happen very often because paper plates are good for about 10,000 impressions and the average job size is only about 1000 impressions. After the job is run, the press operator stacks the printed material on a table for the finishers.

From this point there can be quite a bit of variation in how orders are finished. If the paper needs to be trimmed to a different size, it goes to the paper cutter. If pages need to be collated, they go to the collator and, usually, a binding operation. Binding can take several different forms, many of which can be done in the shop. Any perfect binding, however, needs to be sent to an outside contractor who has a minimum lead time of two days. Finally, the order is prepared for either pick up by or delivery to the customer. There are three full-time shop employees who do only the finishing work. This work is relatively unskilled, and Jon has never had any trouble finding plenty of young people willing to do the finishing work. The front counter people handle all of the customer pick ups and consolidate those orders that are to be delivered. Most of the work is picked up by customers.

About one-quarter of the jobs require additional steps. If a job requires more than one color ink, the job may need to make two passes through the press. Only one of Jon's three presses, a rebuilt AB Dick 375, is currently set up to print two colors simultaneously. If the job has more than one paper stock, for example, a book with cover and pages of different weights, it requires two completely different setups. This may be done on the same press, but it doesn't have to be. Jon has always believed in having one operator for each press to give him the maximum scheduling flexibility so jobs could be run concurrently. Although one operator can run two presses, each press has a distinct personality. There are currently two AB Dick 375 presses in the shop that look identical, yet they operate quite differently. The differences are great enough, Jon believes, to make specialization almost mandatory.

Each job must also have a plate made from the camera-ready original material. The process is quite simple if the original is camera-ready. All of Jon's presses use either a traditional metal plate or a paper plate, which is quick and inexpensive to make. The print quality is equal to that of a metal plate, but it doesn't last as long. However, paper plates cannot be reused. A metal plate can be stored if a job is to be run again in the near future. Paper plates are made on a machine on the shop floor. The machine looks like a big copy machine and is just as easy to operate. For the longer runs the shop can make metal plates, but this requires processing in the darkroom. A blank metal plate is exposed and developed using a photographic process.

Jon pushed back his chair and looked out his office window at the mountains. "If I decide to change procedures and the layout in the shop," he thought, "there are going to be major hassles. But if it would make a difference, it might be worth it. I can't afford any dissatisfied customers."

CASE **3**

PDQ Printing: Forecasting and Capacity

"Sometimes you can have too much of a good thing. I bought this business because I was sure it would provide an adequate living, but I never expected the kind of growth we have experienced. I wonder what next year is going to bring?" These were the thoughts running through the mind of Jon Dominick, the owner of PDQ Printing, as he sat down to do his annual planning. The fiscal year had just ended, and it had been a big success. Sales and profits were both up considerably. His twelfth year in business had been his best ever, and the prospects for next year looked just as bright.

In August 1979 Jon purchased a three-year-old printing business in Evergreen, Colorado. He had spent over a month thoroughly analyzing the local business community and investigating this business before he purchased it. He talked to customers, both satisfied and dissatisfied, and to competitors of PDQ. Although the revenue was a modest $80,000, the margins looked good and Jon thought he saw several areas where the business could be expanded with minimal effort. By 1985 the business had grown to about $500,000 gross revenue. A new press, other support equipment, and additional employees had been added. Jon remembers those first five or six years, not so fondly, as a frantic effort to satisfy every customer who came in the door. It was a tremendous task to keep up, and they often fell behind schedule. The overall objective during those first few years was to expand the business. In retrospect, they had accepted quite a bit of work they should not have. They were, and still are, best equipped to run general-purpose jobs in one or two colors of a modest length, about 1000 copies. They will do longer runs, but such jobs are the exception rather than the rule. Anything with more than two colors or any sophisticated bindings must be subcontracted.

For the next three years, the business grew at a more modest rate to about $600,000 total revenue. Some equipment was added, but most of the effort went into rebuilding existing equipment and consolidating the operation. During this period, the shop tried to concentrate more and more on its core business, and, in general, things began to run progressively smoother. Jon did try to expand by buying an existing print shop in Aspen Park that did about the same type of jobs. For nearly five years he ran it as a satellite operation. It was never really profitable, and Jon closed it in 1988. Most of its work was brought into the main facility.

In 1987 Jon had attempted to diversify by purchasing a small commercial printing business that did magazines and books. This form of high-volume, multicolor printing was quite a bit different from PDQ's main business. This attempt at diversification had come to a startlingly quick and unusual end. The former owners of the commercial operation violated a noncompeting business clause in the purchase contract and were forced to take the business back and pay a penalty. At any rate, Jon decided that diversification was not a good idea. The commercial print shop just took time and energy away from the operation at PDQ. The current business at PDQ was and still is going far better than he had expected, and he doesn't see any reason to mess with success.

The past two years have exceeded all plans and expectations. Gross revenues now exceed $800,000, and all the presses are operating at full capacity. Jon knows that if he doesn't plan his next moves correctly, the company will find itself scrambling to keep up as it had during the first few years he owned it. He doesn't want to live through those times again (see Table 1).

It seems clear to Jon that he needs a new press. He still has the same AB Dick press that was the heart of the business when he bought it. It was rebuilt in 1988, and, at that time, a T-head was installed so that the press could do two-color printing. About seven years ago, he had picked up a second, rebuilt AB Dick press essentially just like the one he already had. This press was only equipped for one-color printing. When he closed the Aspen Park shop, he brought the old AB Dick automated system from that shop to Evergreen. Although this press could print and bind in one operation, it was old, slow, and only did one color. In its current state, the press was capable of a maximum of 5000 impressions per day. "Impressions" is Jon's measure of capacity. This is essentially the number of sheets of paper that can be run through a press in a normal 8-hour work day after allowing for setups and maintenance. About two years ago, Jon had purchased dedicated binding equipment

TABLE 1   PDQ Printing Income Statement. 1991

Account	Debit	Credit
Income		
Sales		$842,000
Other		4,050
Interest		1,730
Expenses		
Supplies—paper	$182,000	
Printing supplies	40,500	
Outside printing	56,400	
Graphics	61,800	
Advertising	1,475	
Auto/truck gas	2,240	
Auto/truck maint.	1,200	
Bank & credit charges	580	
Equipment rental	42	
Insurance	14,050	
Interest	6,500	
Legal & accounting	325	
Misc.	30	
Off. supplies & postage	5,210	
Freight	2,560	
Rent	34,000	
Repairs & maint.—equipment	24,300	
Salaries	297,875	
Taxes—payroll	21,240	
Taxes—sales	24,525	
Taxes—other	2,250	
State income tax	290	
Telephone	8,640	
Utilities	3,990	
Total	$792,022	$847,780
Profit (loss)		$ 55,758

(continued)

TABLE 1   (continued)   1990

Account	Debit	Credit
Income		
Sales		$722,650
Other		3,600
Interest		1,540
Expenses		
Supplies—paper	$156,760	
Printing supplies	35,900	
Outside printing	67,840	
Graphics	55,360	
Advertising	1,410	
Auto/truck gas	1,925	
Auto/truck maint.	980	
Bank & credit charges	480	
Equipment rental	40	
Insurance	11,580	
Interest	5,600	
Legal & accounting	470	
Misc.	25	
Off. supplies & postage	4,450	
Freight	2,180	
Rent	33,600	
Repairs & maint.—equipment	20,950	
Proceeds/sale of assets		1,800
Salaries	239,600	
Taxes—payroll	17,990	
Taxes—sales	21,800	
Taxes—other	2,070	
State income tax	258	
Federal income tax	(815)	
Telephone	7,440	
Utilities	3,540	
Total	$691,433	$729,590
Profit (loss)		$ 38,157

(continued)

TABLE 1 (continued) 1989

Account	Debit	Credit
Income		
Sales		$635,400
Other		200
Interest		1,140
Expenses		
Supplies—paper	$122,425	
Printing supplies	38,845	
Outside printing	62,610	
Graphics	32,618	
Advertising	590	
Auto/truck gas	1,800	
Auto/truck maint.	1,125	
Bank & credit charges	480	
Insurance	8,800	
Interest	3,500	
Legal & accounting	670	
Misc	12	
Off. supplies & postage	3,000	
Freight	2,050	
Rent	33,450	
Repairs & maint.—equipment	14,720	
Salaries	225,160	
Proceeds/sale of assets		10,780
Taxes—payroll	17,100	
Taxes—sales	19,765	
Taxes—other	3,925	
Telephone	6,345	
Utilities	3,260	
Total	$602,250	$647,520
Profit (loss)		$ 45,270

(continued)

TABLE 1   (continued)   1988

Account	Debit	Credit
Income		
Sales		$579,170
Other		2,450
Interest		4,890
Expenses		
Supplies—paper	$116,220	
Printing supplies	30,940	
Outside printing	47,960	
Advertising	1,375	
Auto/truck gas	1,700	
Auto/truck maint.	630	
Bank & credit charges	695	
Insurance	7,320	
Contract labor	4,800	
Interest	5,530	
Legal & accounting	2,530	
Off. supplies & postage	2,280	
Freight	1,850	
Rent	30,140	
Repairs & maint.—equipment	14,000	
Salaries	216,225	
Proceeds/sale of assets		2,840
Taxes—payroll	21,115	
Taxes—sales	18,975	
Taxes—other	4,680	
Telephone	6,990	
Utilities	2,230	
Moving expense	1,222	
Total	$539,407	$589,350
Profit (loss)		$ 49,943

that was faster, more flexible, of higher quality, and more reliable than the AB Dick system. Jon has decided that when he buys a new press, he will get rid of the AB Dick automated system. He now faces the question of which new press to buy. He has been to some local printers and equipment distributors to investigate the current marketplace and has narrowed the decision to three different presses.

One possibility is to purchase a new AB Dick 375 just like the two he already has. This press is a reliable performer, and everyone in the shop is, of course, quite familiar with its operation. It can handle up to 13" x 17" stock and can be purchased with a T-head to do two-color printing. It is capable of about 18,000 single-sided impressions per day. Their current 375s have served them well for many years. Setups are relatively easy, and the press is well suited to their current business. The 375 is an adequate performer that maintains good, but not great, registration of the plates. "Registration" is a measure of the ability of a press to exactly align multiple impressions on the same paper. This is quite important in jobs requiring more than two colors. Any misalignment results in gaps in color or the printing of one color on top of another. The AB Dick can run both metal and paper plates, which offers some flexibility. Paper plates generally are good for about 10,000 impressions, and metal plates can last for 30,000 impressions but are much more expensive to make. Although the familiarity with the press seems like a strong positive attribute, Jon has been in the printing business long enough to know that, no matter how similar two presses may be, each press has a distinct personality. Two presses might seem identical on the surface but run quite differently. A new two-color 375 would cost $20,000.

The second alternative is to purchase a Hamada press. Jon has seen this unit at several large commercial printers in the area and is quite intrigued. It is a two-color press with a very sophisticated paper-handling system that maintains excellent registration during a run. It is capable of very long runs and can handle 18" × 24" sheets of paper. It is designed to use only metal plates because paper plates would not hold up for long runs. It uses a molleton printing technology, which contributes to its high performance but makes clean up and setup considerably more difficult and time consuming (see Table 2). This technology also requires the use of oil-based inks. Jon estimates that the Hamada is capable of 20,000 impressions. A Hamada can be purchased for $30,000.

The third alternative is an Itek Perfector. Jon knows of this press only by reputation and advertisement because it is new in the marketplace and none of the local firms have one. The distributor will be receiving one in a few weeks. Itek has a very good reputation in the field, and Jon already has an Itek paper plate maker that works just fine. However, the plate maker and the press are actually made for Itek by two different companies. The Itek is also a two-color press but, unlike the others, prints two sides simultaneously. PDQ does some two-sided jobs, and the Itek would certainly run those jobs more efficiently than

TABLE 2   Printing Technologies

Printing Basics

Essentially, printing relies on the fact that oil and water do not mix. A combination of ink and water is applied to the plate. The inks can be oil based, rubber based, or soy based. The ink adheres to the image areas, and the water fills the nonimage areas. The plate transfers the ink to a mat that is pressed against the paper, and the image is printed. The paper must then dry before trimming, binding, or other finishing tasks can be performed.

Molleton Technology

The ink and water are completely separate through the entire process. The water is applied by a first set of rollers—rubber rollers covered with a molleton, a felt sock that evenly applies the water. The ink is applied by a second set of rollers. Oil-based inks must be used, and they cannot stand open for long before they begin to dry. They do, however, dry faster on the paper. This process is used by all high-volume commercial printers. Both sets of rollers must be removed and cleaned between jobs.

Integrated Technology

The ink and water are mixed in the machine and applied to the plate by one set of rollers. Rubber-based inks are often used, and they can stand open for long periods of time (overnight) providing considerable flexibility in press operation. However, rubber-based inks are slower to dry and are not generally used on glossy paper. Oil- and soy-based inks may be used. Only one set of rollers must be cleaned between jobs, and there is no real difference in clean up time for the different inks.

---

the 375s. As it stands now, two-sided jobs have to be run through the press twice. Jon estimates that this press would have a capacity of 25,000 two-sided impressions, and it can use 13" x 17" paper. It uses the same integrated technology as the AB Dick presses in the shop now, which implies a relatively easy clean up. It also means that the shop can continue to use mostly rubber-based inks. The ability of rubber-based inks to remain exposed on the press for long periods allows a great deal of scheduling flexibility. Setup and registration on the Itek are question marks without actually working on the press. However, the marketing literature and reports that Jon has seen in trade journals claim these are excellent. Jon has spent some time negotiating with the distributor and feels he can get this press for about $32,000. This is a substantial discount because the distributor is anxious to get a press in a local shop.

Whichever press Jon decides to buy, he will have to train the current AB Dick automated press operator on the new equipment. His policy is to have one press operator for each press. He has investigated layout options that allow one operator to run two presses, but he feels he sacrifices productivity in these layouts. This is primarily due to the personality differences between presses, which are generally great enough to reward specialization. Including vacation and other benefits, a new press operator will cost Jon $25,000 annually. The shop is currently running one 9-hour shift per day. With breaks and lunch, this works out to about 8 hours of productive time per employee per shift. Any overtime is paid at time and one half, but Jon does not encourage the practice. He feels overtime reduces productivity and morale, and it is used only in crisis situations. The shop now runs about 250 days a year.

The decision to buy a new press is based on Jon's forecast for the next three years. Frankly, this is a pretty intuitive process. Jon certainly has learned a considerable amount about the printing business in the past twelve years and feels his sense of the business and the marketplace is accurate. Most of the work at PDQ is small- to medium-length runs (in the range of 100 to 5000 pieces) of flyers, pamphlets, brochures, letterhead, posters, advertisements, and other such jobs. The shop runs about 40 jobs per day, averaging about 1000 impressions per job, with an occasional run of over 10,000. Jon expects this business to continue to grow. He has established a sound reputation for high quality, good service, and reasonable prices and correctly feels this contributes strongly to the growth of the company. In fact, Jon has not raised prices in four years. PDQ essentially operates on a debt-free basis, and Jon feels he can finance the purchase of a new press with the revenue from operations.

"Now," Jon thought, "what should I do about this press decision?"

COMPANY 5

SALT RIVER LABS

CASE **A**   Salt River Labs: Introduction to Operations Management

John Saunders started work at Salt River Labs on February 1 as Vice-President of Production. Salt River Labs is an analytical testing laboratory that has three basic laboratory operations, Industrial Hygiene, Environmental, and Asbestos. Last year Salt River essentially broke even on $2.4 million in sales. They employ 55 people in one location in Tempe, Arizona.

John spent the first day trying to learn as much about the Industrial Hygiene lab as possible. He talked to Georgia Hoffman (President), Dennis Farina (Manager of Industrial Hygiene), and Marta Allison (Supervisor of Industrial Hygiene's Organic Analysis section). After each meeting he went back to his office and made some notes to try to capture the essence of the conversation. At the end of the day, he threw all the notes in his briefcase and headed for home. After dinner he sat down in front of the fireplace to review the notes and prepare for the next day.

NOTES FROM MEETING WITH GEORGIA HOFFMAN

Spoke with Georgia Hoffman for about an hour. She is very concerned that the "output from the lab isn't very good." She clearly thinks the chemists aren't working very hard. She believes they are "working against due date"—that is, they do enough each day to keep up with the volume of work coming in, but they don't work hard enough to reduce the WIP (work in process, the dollar value of the work in house).

129

"Look, there's $40,000 on the WIP, and they only billed out about $8000 yesterday and $5000 the day before. We logged in (received) $14,000 yesterday and $10,000 the day before. I don't think they do anything until a job is due, and then they miss the due date a lot of the time."

Georgia focuses intently on the daily billings as a measure of effort put forth by the laboratory the day before. The first thing she does each morning is check the billing total from the previous day. Frequently she goes "over (to the lab) to encourage them and try to motivate them a little bit. But it just doesn't seem to have any effect."

She explained that she wanted me to develop a "better scheduling system so that we can get more out." She called Marta Allison into her office (summoned is probably a more appropriate term) to introduce her to me. Told Marta Allison that I would be doing the scheduling for Industrial Hygiene to try to "make things flow smoother."

NOTES FROM MEETING WITH MARTA ALLISON

Marta Allison informed me that she is "from the old school" and felt uncomfortable talking with me before I "have talked with her boss" (Dennis Farina). I told her that seemed entirely reasonable to me and got up to leave, but then we talked for about a half hour.

Marta doesn't understand (resents?) being called into Georgia Hoffman's office without Dennis Farina. "It just isn't right. Is she (Georgia Hoffman) trying to tell me something? Is she telling me I'm going to be fired?"

Marta seems friendly enough—a straight shooter. We talked about who's-who, who-does-what, past history of Salt River, the number of "good people" who have left or been fired, and several things that she thinks should be done better. Once she starts, she is hard to stop. We finally agreed that I should come back to talk with her after I had talked with Dennis Farina.

NOTES FROM MEETING WITH DENNIS FARINA

Dennis Farina seems like a very open and honest guy. There are things he "won't tell me" (at least not until he knows me better), but he was straight forward about that. (The things he "won't tell me" seem to relate to company actions of which he doesn't approve. Hmmm. Follow up later.)

He asked me what I was doing here. He had not been informed that I was being hired (although he had heard it through the grapevine). After I described my role (even I am not very clear on that), he stated that he agreed that we could use some help scheduling, but that (a) there are other matters that are more important, and (b) "good luck" getting Marta to give that up. It seems that Marta and another supervisor do the scheduling for the chemists who work for them.

Dennis spent some time explaining the process flow and physical layout for Salt River Labs. He sketched out a flowchart (see Figure 1) on the marker board which I copied down, and he took me on a quick tour of the facilities (see Figure 2).

We did discuss some of the "other matters." (I think I have a headache.) Things I learned:

Payrolls are not being met on time. On paydays (every other Friday) Georgia comes around to ask who can wait until next week to be paid. Sometimes some people get paid and others don't (until later); other times everyone (except "volunteers") gets a partial payment of $100 to $200. The remaining pay usually, but not always, is delivered by Tuesday of the next week.

There is a lot of antipathy between the lab and the marketing people. Dennis complained bitterly about the apparent policy of "selling anything they can, even if we can't do it or if it will disrupt our production flow." The lab work typically consists of lots of very small jobs that require separate setups for analysis. One way of minimizing the number of setups is to wait until a number of small jobs with similar analyses have been collected and then to run them together as a "batch." However, the salespeople frequently promise the small jobs on a "3 day rush" (or even on 24- or 48-hour rush), which prevents effective batching. Normal turnaround time for jobs is seven days (ten days on certain analyses). Dennis is also concerned that this kind of activity pressures the chemists to "cut corners," which may result in inaccurate analysis and reports.

Dennis also complained about pricing. "Management is always talking about 'invoiced amounts' and the amount of work that 'came in yesterday' (measured in standard price list value) and the amount of work 'on the WIP.' They don't realize that what came in yesterday won't go out for six or seven working days." He believes that management doesn't know how a lab operates. Further, they ignore the fact that, on average, jobs only invoice out at 90% of their listed value. Dennis strongly (I mean *strongly*) believes that our pricing is completely messed up: we are underpriced on many analyses, we should have a minimum charge for "onesies and twosies," and we shouldn't be selling some types of analyses at all.

Figure 1   *Salt River Labs Flowchart*

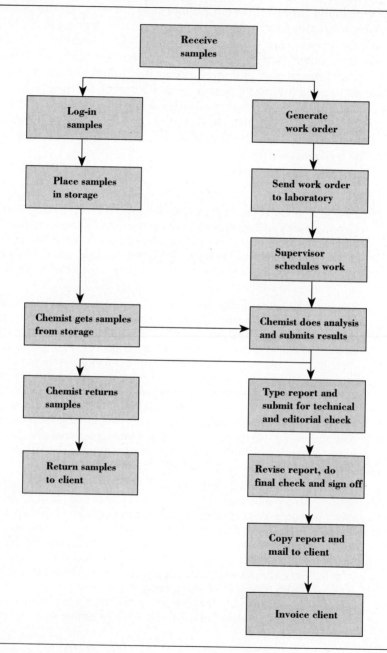

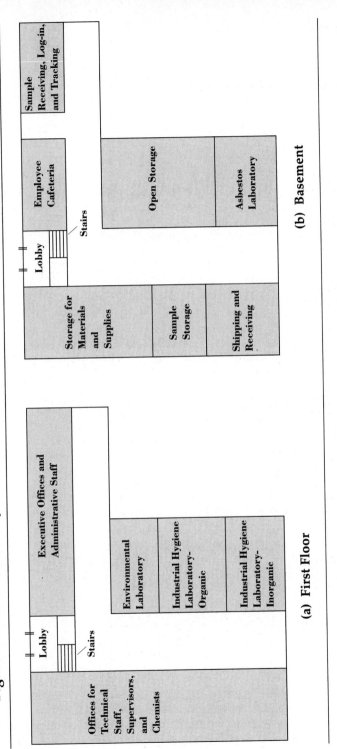

Figure 2 Salt River Labs Layout: (a) First Floor; (b) Basement

133

Equipment is not maintained. Although the chemists can do simple routine maintenance and make minor repairs, Dennis believes that we should have a service contract with Hewlett-Packard (HP). We used to have one, but dropped it because "it costs too much" (Georgia's words and decision). Apparently we owe HP a considerable amount of money. (Dennis doesn't know how much, but "it's a lot" and they have a court judgment against us.)

We often don't have the chemicals, glassware, or other supplies to do the work in time. Actually it may be more accurate to say we can't find the equipment or supplies. All such material is stored in the basement of the building in open racks. Anyone who needs anything goes downstairs and picks it off the shelf. There is no real order to the storage, and items are randomly placed on the shelves as they are received by whomever happens to be assigned that job that day.

Several former suppliers won't do business with us any longer. This is apparently because we owe them money. Purchasing is done by Susie Martinez, an asbestos analyst who devotes two half-days per week to it. Dennis thinks she tries hard, but she doesn't have enough time or enough knowledge and experience to do it very well. They used to have a woman doing purchasing and inventory full time, but Georgia fired her "to cut costs." Although the situation has deteriorated since she left, it was not good even when she was here.

NOTES FROM MEETING WITH MARTA ALLISON

Talked again with Marta (after I had been "cleared by Dennis Farina"). It is evident that Marta has enormous respect for Dennis—not just as a boss, but as a person and a friend. Marta and Dennis have been at Salt River for over twelve years and were hired by the original owner, Dan Glover. Apparently Georgia Hoffman bought the business from Glover about three years ago after having worked there for six months as VP of Finance.

She does seem hostile to my being introduced as a scheduler. (Why not? She's been doing this herself for several years.) I decided to stay away from that subject for a while and asked her to describe any production problems ("barriers or impediments to getting work out"). Bingo! She was ready to tell me everything.

She showed me three jobs that are already late because her chemists don't have the standards or chemicals necessary to do the analyses. These are standards and chemicals that should always be on hand. She put in a requisition for them, but they have not been received. They were ordered, but not in time. It's not Susie Martinez's fault. "She only does purchasing part time and they don't give her any money to buy things until it's too late." (Apparently the acquisition of supplies and materials just does not happen until something has "gone critical.")

One of the gas chromatographs (GC) with an autosampler (which allows the GC to run overnight with automatic injection and analysis of samples) was set up to run 50 samples last night, but it stopped about an hour after the chemist left for the day. (Fifty samples represents $2500 at an average billing rate of about $50 per sample.) This is not an unusual occurrence; it happens frequently. Neither Marta nor her chemists know why this is happening. They have asked for repair and maintenance service but have been told that we can't afford it.

Only two of the four GCs have autosamplers on them. With an autosampler, a chemist can prepare and set up as many as 80 samples to run unattended (assuming the instrument doesn't malfunction). It takes about 20 minutes to "shoot" (that is, for the GC to analyze) each sample. Additionally each "run" of several samples must also include quality control samples (no charge), standards (for instrument calibration), and "blanks" (for quality control and determining baselines for quantifying the amounts of compounds detected in the samples). On average, these number about 25% of the number of billable samples. When I later asked Georgia Hoffman about acquiring additional autosamplers, she responded "we can't afford it" and with suggestions that the chemists are "cry babies" and "prima donnas" who just don't want to do sample injections by hand.

It is clear that serving the customer is very important to Marta, and she tries very had to schedule work according to the order in which it was received. She perceives this as very fair. Occasionally there are large contract orders which she handles differently. They are moved to the front of the queue.

Marta's concern for the customer came out in another way. It seems that she suspects one of the new chemists of "faking" test results and turning in data without doing the actual work. Marta doesn't have any control over hire/fire decisions (these are apparently all Georgia's) and feels she has no control over this problem. Apparently there is no system in place to monitor the performance of chemists to prevent problems like this from occurring.

Marta clearly had much more to say, but we had to cut the meeting off at this point. I guess I'll get more tomorrow.

John sits back, looks into the glowing embers of the fire, and considers the problems he discovered today. After a long time, he begins to make notes for tomorrow.

CASE 1

Salt River Labs: Quality and Productivity

John Saunders sat at his desk on Friday afternoon. It was the end of his first week on the job at Salt River Labs. He looked at the papers spread out before him and considered his plans for the coming week. His first few days were spent talking to the key people in the various areas of the company. After that, he had concentrated on gathering information on issues concerning the quality of service provided by SRL and the true productivity of the laboratory.

One of the things bothering John was that there didn't seem to be much concern about productivity. There was plenty of concern about keeping costs down—so much concern, he believed, that SRL's production capabilities were severely handicapped and that revenues and profits were being adversely affected. There was certainly lots of pressure to "get the jobs out," but there wasn't much effort to relate the costs of production to the amount or results of production.

Arthur Gregory, the Senior VP–Finance, had given him all kinds of data and charts tracking and comparing revenues over the last two years (Table 1). None of them contained any information about the number or types of analyses performed nor about what prices had been charged or how the prices may have changed over that time. Similarly Arthur had given John several pages of data and charts about how, in his words, "costs have gotten completely out of hand." Although Arthur broke the total cost of sales down by laboratory (Industrial Hygiene, Environmental, and Microscopy), he didn't look at the component parts of cost of sales (labor, materials, other), nor did he break them down by product line, function, or use. In fact he was unable to provide any in-

TABLE 1 Income Statement 1989

GROSS PROFIT MARGINS

	JAN	FEB	MAR	APR	MAY	JUN	JUL	AUG	SEP	OCT	NOV	DEC	TOTAL
MICROSCOPY													
Sales Revenues	69,134	50,734	51,938	48,127	38,994	44,082	30,921	49,117	24,265	28,889	16,084	30,741	483,026
Cost of Sales	16,660	14,600	16,730	14,885	16,902	16,612	15,880	16,799	15,244	15,057	14,019	15,308	188,696
Gross Profit	52,474	36,134	35,208	33,242	22,092	27,470	15,041	32,318	9,021	13,832	2,065	15,433	294,330
Gross Profit Margin	75.9%	71.2%	67.8%	69.1%	56.7%	62.3%	48.6%	65.8%	37.2%	47.9%	12.8%	50.2%	60.9%
INDUSTRIAL HYGIENE													
Sales Revenues	55,531	56,907	75,950	63,841	87,984	107,778	77,380	88,911	122,238	92,588	87,531	74,446	991,085
Cost of Sales	36,191	36,784	38,102	26,937	31,587	31,669	31,929	33,490	37,453	36,366	37,216	32,491	410,215
Gross Profit	19,340	20,123	37,848	36,904	56,397	76,109	45,451	55,421	84,785	56,222	50,315	41,955	580,870
Gross Profit Margin	34.8%	35.4%	49.8%	57.8%	64.1%	70.6%	58.7%	62.3%	69.4%	60.7%	57.5%	56.4%	58.6%
ENVIRONMENTAL													
Sales Revenues	30,825	19,373	28,020	29,692	32,313	14,391	9,282	15,285	16,814	20,100	24,280	58,039	298,414
Cost of Sales	42,643	43,758	45,706	27,569	27,250	21,168	22,709	19,475	21,673	25,484	29,152	22,719	349,306
Gross Profit	(11,818)	(24,385)	(17,686)	2,123	5,063	(6,777)	(13,427)	(4,190)	(4,859)	(5,384)	(4,872)	35,320	(50,892)
Gross Profit Margin	-38.3%	-125.9%	-63.1%	7.2%	15.7%	-47.1%	-144.7%	-27.4%	-28.9%	-26.8%	-20.1%	60.9%	-17.1%
LABORATORY TOTAL													
Sales Revenues	155,490	127,014	155,908	141,660	159,291	166,251	117,583	153,313	163,317	141,577	127,895	163,226	1,772,525
Cost of Sales	95,494	95,142	100,538	69,391	75,739	69,449	70,518	69,764	74,370	76,907	80,387	70,518	948,217
Gross Profit	59,996	31,872	55,370	72,269	83,552	96,802	47,065	83,549	88,947	64,670	47,508	92,708	824,308
Gross Profit Margin	38.6%	25.1%	35.5%	51.0%	52.5%	58.2%	40.0%	54.5%	54.5%	45.7%	37.1%	56.8%	46.5%
NON-LABORATORY OTHER													
Sales Revenues	9,554	9,076	12,835	15,040	18,697	12,030	8,375	699	1,316	9,153	2,222	2,001	100,998
Cost of Sales	22,532	12,123	18,617	17,314	20,370	21,013	17,892	19,268	19,479	18,610	21,053	18,954	227,225
Gross Profit	(12,978)	(3,047)	(5,782)	(2,274)	(1,673)	(8,983)	(9,517)	(18,569)	(18,163)	(9,457)	(18,831)	(16,953)	(126,227)
Gross Profit Margin	-135.8%	-33.6%	-45.0%	-15.1%	-8.9%	-74.7%	-113.6%	-2656.5%	-1380.2%	-103.3%	-847.5%	-847.2%	-125.0%
LAB+NONLAB TOTAL													
Sales Revenues	165,044	136,090	168,743	156,700	177,988	178,281	125,958	154,012	164,633	150,730	130,117	165,227	1,873,523
Cost of Sales	118,026	107,265	119,155	86,705	96,109	90,462	88,410	89,032	93,849	95,517	101,440	89,472	1,175,442
Gross Profit	47,018	28,825	49,588	69,995	81,879	87,819	37,548	64,980	70,784	55,213	28,677	75,755	698,081
Gross Profit Margin	28.5%	21.2%	29.4%	44.7%	46.0%	49.3%	29.8%	42.2%	43.0%	36.6%	22.0%	45.8%	37.3%

(continued)

TABLE 1 (continued) 1989

	JAN	FEB	MAR	APR	MAY	JUN	JUL	AUG	SEP	OCT	NOV	DEC	TOTAL
OPERATING EXPENSES													
Customer Service	15,967	15,531	20,961	13,466	13,053	12,123	11,953	9,872	9,861	10,991	11,185	12,000	156,963
Sales/Marketing	31,349	40,500	41,757	9,405	13,142	16,504	12,424	14,188	11,439	21,122	15,571	20,000	247,401
General & Admin.	90,159	67,431	83,960	65,956	74,696	66,773	120,189	85,655	78,837	82,287	81,448	82,400	979,791
Depreciation	1,701	1,701	1,701	1,701	1,701	1,701	1,701	1,651	1,651	1,651	1,651	1,651	20,162
Bad Debt Expense	500	500	500	500	500	500	500	500	1,922	500	500	500	7,422
Repairs & Maint.													0
Total	139,676	125,663	148,879	91,028	103,092	97,601	146,767	111,866	103,710	116,551	110,355	116,551	1,411,739
PROFIT (LOSS) BEFORE INTEREST & TAXES	(92,658)	(96,838)	(99,291)	(21,033)	(21,213)	(9,782)	(109,219)	(46,886)	(32,926)	(61,338)	(81,678)	(40,796)	(713,658)
OTHER INCOME/EXPENSE													
Interest Income/Exp	(14,970)	(17,981)	(11,457)	(11,016)	(11,031)	(11,045)	(36,039)	(19,631)	(18,785)	(17,330)	(17,231)	(18,000)	(204,516)
Miscellaneous	(8,176)	(381)	9	(1,686)	(290)	(880)	(244,389)	(511)	(6,209)	1,030			(261,483)
Total	(23,146)	(18,362)	(11,448)	(12,702)	(11,321)	(11,925)	(280,428)	(20,142)	(24,994)	(16,300)	(17,231)	(18,000)	(465,999)
NET INCOME (LOSS) BEFORE TAXES	(115,804)	(115,200)	(110,739)	(33,735)	(32,534)	(21,707)	(389,647)	(67,028)	(57,920)	(77,638)	(98,909)	(58,796)	(1,179,657)

(continued)

139

TABLE 1 (continued) Income Statement 1988

	JAN	FEB	MAR	APR	MAY	JUN	JUL	AUG	SEP	OCT	NOV	DEC	TOTAL
GROSS PROFIT MARGINS													
MICROSCOPY													
Sales Revenues	62,788	49,561	59,569	57,048	56,981	58,697	40,274	46,806	49,949	38,788	32,834	42,661	595,957
Cost of Sales	15,840	13,800	16,135	14,322	15,483	15,891	15,101	15,327	15,579	15,033	14,946	15,128	182,585
Gross Profit	46,948	35,761	43,434	42,726	41,498	42,806	25,173	31,479	34,370	23,755	17,888	27,533	413,372
Gross Profit Margin	74.8%	72.2%	72.9%	74.9%	72.8%	72.9%	62.5%	67.3%	68.8%	61.2%	54.5%	64.5%	69.4%
INDUSTRIAL HYGIENE													
Sales Revenues	157,269	128,965	152,348	136,720	145,541	140,670	96,519	112,173	112,913	85,768	69,103	90,256	1,428,246
Cost of Sales	36,296	35,352	36,188	35,777	34,680	34,481	32,017	33,589	34,803	34,106	36,558	37,279	421,126
Gross Profit	120,973	93,613	116,160	100,943	110,861	106,189	64,502	78,584	78,110	51,662	32,545	52,977	1,007,120
Gross Profit Margin	76.9%	72.6%	76.2%	73.8%	76.2%	75.5%	66.8%	70.1%	69.2%	60.2%	47.1%	58.7%	70.5%
ENVIRONMENTAL													
Sales Revenues	57,437	46,597	60,356	50,575	62,948	52,036	35,704	41,495	42,508	28,727	21,562	28,387	528,334
Cost of Sales	40,104	40,001	44,312	43,119	45,271	43,375	41,953	42,238	41,850	40,782	40,052	40,791	503,848
Gross Profit	17,333	6,596	16,044	7,456	17,677	8,661	(6,249)	(743)	658	(12,055)	(18,490)	(12,404)	24,486
Gross Profit Margin	30.2%	14.2%	26.6%	14.7%	28.1%	16.6%	-17.5%	-1.8%	1.5%	-42.0%	-85.7%	-43.7%	4.6%
LABORATORY TOTAL													
Sales Revenues	277,495	225,123	272,274	244,343	265,471	251,404	172,496	200,474	205,370	153,283	123,499	161,305	2,552,536
Cost of Sales	92,240	89,153	96,635	93,218	95,434	93,747	89,071	91,154	92,232	89,921	91,556	93,198	1,107,559
Gross Profit	185,255	135,970	175,639	151,125	170,037	157,657	83,425	109,320	113,138	63,362	31,943	68,107	1,444,977
Gross Profit Margin	66.8%	60.4%	64.5%	61.8%	64.1%	62.7%	48.4%	54.5%	55.1%	41.3%	25.9%	42.2%	56.6%
NON-LABORATORY OTHER													
Sales Revenues	10,481	8,503	10,284	9,229	10,027	9,495	6,515	7,572	7,757	5,789	4,665	6,092	96,409
Cost of Sales	14,877	13,661	14,222	14,748	17,590	18,128	19,810	19,533	17,107	17,599	17,841	18,549	203,665
Gross Profit	(4,396)	(5,158)	(3,938)	(5,519)	(7,563)	(8,633)	(13,295)	(11,961)	(9,350)	(11,810)	(13,176)	(12,457)	(107,256)
Gross Profit Margin	-41.9%	-60.7%	-38.3%	-59.8%	-75.4%	-90.9%	-204.1%	-158.0%	-120.5%	-204.0%	-282.5%	-204.5%	-111.3%
LAB+NONLAB TOTAL													
Sales Revenues	287,975	233,625	282,557	253,572	275,497	260,899	179,012	208,046	213,127	159,072	128,164	167,397	2,648,945
Cost of Sales	107,117	102,814	110,857	107,966	113,024	111,875	108,881	110,687	109,339	107,520	109,397	111,747	1,311,224
Gross Profit	180,858	130,811	171,700	145,606	162,473	149,024	70,131	97,359	103,788	51,552	18,767	55,650	1,337,721
Gross Profit Margin	62.8%	56.0%	60.8%	57.4%	59.0%	57.1%	39.2%	46.8%	48.7%	32.4%	14.6%	33.2%	50.5%

(continued)

TABLE 1 (continued) 1988

	JAN	FEB	MAR	APR	MAY	JUN	JUL	AUG	SEP	OCT	NOV	DEC	TOTAL
OPERATING EXPENSES													
Customer Service	15,009	15,686	16,978	12,927	13,575	13,457	11,714	10,366	11,340	13,739	14,205	15,120	164,116
Sales/Marketing	20,347	33,593	32,774	28,100	29,798	31,921	36,824	38,507	34,943	35,221	31,290	33,726	387,044
General & Admin.	60,828	55,771	64,489	68,822	74,969	67,737	76,808	82,736	78,378	84,277	84,251	82,005	881,071
Depreciation	1,811	1,811	1,811	1,811	1,811	1,701	1,701	1,651	1,651	1,651	1,651	1,651	20,712
Bad Debt Expense	875	875	875	875	875	875	875	500	500	500	500	1,350	9,475
Repairs & Maint.	925	1,058	750	750	1,275	750	750	1,000	750	0	0	0	8,008
Total	99,795	108,794	117,677	113,285	122,303	116,441	128,672	134,760	127,562	135,388	131,897	133,852	1,470,426
PROFIT (LOSS) BEFORE INTEREST & TAXES	81,063	22,017	54,023	32,320	40,170	32,583	(58,541)	(37,400)	(23,774)	(83,835)	(113,130)	(78,202)	(132,705)
OTHER INCOME/EXPENSE													
Interest Income/Exp	(9,825)	(9,825)	(11,016)	(11,016)	(10,888)	(10,982)	(12,200)	(12,321)	(13,555)	(13,780)	14,290	14,622	(86,496)
Miscellaneous	3,451	(679)	1,274	(42)	(873)	1,667	(42,586)	(737)	(8,339)	1,223	(486)	(2,306)	(48,433)
Total	(6,374)	(10,504)	(9,742)	(11,058)	(11,761)	(9,315)	(54,786)	(13,058)	(21,894)	(12,557)	13,804	12,316	(134,929)
NET INCOME (LOSS) BEFORE TAXES	74,689	11,513	44,281	21,262	28,409	23,268	(113,327)	(50,458)	(45,668)	(96,392)	(99,326)	(65,886)	(267,634)

formation on the prices SRL was paying for supplies and materials other than to say that:

> I think we're paying a lot more for some things than we should. It seems like we're always paying to have stuff shipped to us expedited. And, the prices of chemicals seem to have doubled or tripled in the last year or so.

Following his meeting with Arthur, John had spent a little time trying to dig out some additional information which he thought would be useful. He talked with Chuck Meyers (Senior VP-Marketing) and Dave Fast (Sales Manager) and was able to come up with both new and an old price lists. From Craig Velly (VP-Information Services) he had gotten a listing of the most frequently performed analyses—along with the number of analyses and revenue generated in 1988 and 1989. John was quite surprised at the information that Craig had or could produce if asked. (Why hadn't anyone asked for it before, he wondered?) John had combined this information into a table (Table 2), but he had not had a chance to look at it closely.

TABLE 2   Price List, Volume, and Revenue for Most Common Analyses 1988 and 1989

	1988			1989		
Analyte/Analysis	List Price	Quantity Sold	Actual Revenue	List Price	Quantity Sold	Actual Revenue
Microscopy						
Filters	$30	13,182	$369,868	$25	13,287	$302,279
Bulk	50	4,837	226,089	40	5,020	180,746
Total			595,957			483,026
Industrial Hygiene (Filters, Plugs, Tubes)						
Arsenic (As)	30	2,144	60,461	25	1,523	35,410
Barium (Ba)	15	89	1,255	12	55	601
Cadmium (Cd)	15	373	5,282	12	203	2,273
Chromium (Cr)	15	2,437	33,704	12	1,562	17,563
Lead (Pb)	15	374	5,610	12	212	2,493
Mercury (Hg)	30	69	2,043	25	59	1,375
Selenium (Se)	30	296	8,525	25	226	5,085
Silver (Ag)	15	87	1,274	12	19	215

(continued)

TABLE 2   (continued)

	1988			1989		
Analyte/Analysis	List Price	Quantity Sold	Actual Revenue	List Price	Quantity Sold	Actual Revenue
Silica (Si)	$ 15	1,339	$ 19,683	$ 12	1,132	$ 13,122
Benzene	30	1,433	42,431	25	1,058	25,551
Toluene	30	1,297	38,599	25	1,003	24,373
Ethylene	30	923	27,053	25	927	22,688
Ethyl Benzene	30	861	25,107	25	562	13,109
Xylene	30	774	22,941	25	570	13,495
BTEX	90	928	77,924	75	877	64,131
Ethylene Oxide	30	884	25,539	25	620	14,694
Chloroform	30	720	21,168	25	631	14,371
Methyl Chloroform	30	659	19,553	25	667	16,075
Methylene Chloride	30	597	17,498	25	429	10,628
Methanol	30	517	15,308	25	463	11,193
Isopropyl Alcohol	30	427	12,708	25	387	8,978
Formaldehyde	30	538	15,026	25	417	10,102
Herbicides	250	52	11,895	200	40	7,632
Pesticides/PCBs	200	2,081	388,731	150	1,811	247,473
GC/MS Screen for Organics	300	480	134,352	250	398	90,446
Semivolatile Organics by GC/MS	400	51	18,013	300	35	9,513
Volatile Organics by GC/FID	100	3,427	328,307	85	2,891	233,694
Volatile Organics by GC/MS	250	83	18,260	175	49	7,863
Total			$1,398,248			$924,145
Environmental Samples (Soil/Water)						
Arsenic (As)	$ 35	137	$ 4,651	$ 30	100	$ 3,000
Barium (Ba)	15	0	0	12	0	0
BTEX	125	914	111,165	90	622	45,344
Cadmium (Cd)	15	0	0	12	0	0
Chloride	15	251	3,716	15	197	2,819
Chromium (Cr)	15	125	1,787	12	43	516
Cyanide	35	112	3,755	30	84	2,948

(continued)

TABLE 2 (continued)

Analyte/Analysis	1988			1989		
	List Price	Quantity Sold	Actual Revenue	List Price	Quantity Sold	Actual Revenue
GC/MS Screen for Organics	$400	98	$ 37,946	$300	77	$ 20,790
Herbicides	250	257	61,250	225	192	38,491
Lead (Pb)	15	255	3,668	12	84	1,008
Mercury (Hg)	35	118	4,014	30	61	1,701
Nitrate/Nitrite	15	183	2,652	15	222	3,230
Pesticides/PCBs	200	419	77,264	150	277	39,597
pH	10	771	7,325	8	513	4,051
RCRA-8 (Ag,As,Ba, Cd,Cr,Hg,Pb,Se)	250	292	68,109	220	213	40,909
Selenium	35	97	3,225	30	66	1,913
Semivolatile Organics by GC/MS	400	128	46,848	300	103	28,768
Silica (Si)	15	282	4,230	12	88	1,056
Silver (Ag)	15	23	345	12	23	276
Total Petroleum Hydrocarbons	60	587	32,015	50	353	15,303
Volatile Organics by GC/MS	250	190	43,273	175	241	39,223
Total			$517,237			$290,942

John also spent a couple hours with Barbara Bensen in accounting. Barbara handled both the accounts receivable and the accounts payable. She worked under the direct supervision of Linda Lacy, the Supervisor of Accounting, who reported to Paul Jensen, the Controller, who reported to Arthur. With Barbara's help, John was able to obtain a sample of vendor invoices for supplies and materials purchased and a sample of SRL invoices for analytic services sold over the last two years. He had summarized the information from these invoices in a table (Table 3).

It seemed clear to John that SRL could benefit from a better understanding of its true productivity. He had some big plans cooking for SRL, and he would need to get everyone thinking about productivity, committed to improving productivity, and actually taking actions to making changes to bring about improvement. Without accurate, appropriate productivity measures, he would never know the true effects of the antici-

TABLE 3 Prices Paid for Key Supplies – 1988 and 1989 (Based on Samples of Invoices Paid)

Material/Supply	Unit of Measure	1988		1989		1990	
		Cost per Unit	Quantity (Units)	Cost per Unit	Quantity (Units)	Cost per Unit	Quantity (Units)
2 ml vials	Box of 100	$ 25.00	0	$ 30.00	14	$ 33.00	
	Case of 5 Boxes	85.00	8	100.00	22	110.00	
	Case (5 or more)	70.00	~~30~~	85.00	10	95.00	
3M Badges	Each	1.75	0	1.90	125	2.20	
	Box of 100	140.00	0	150.00	14	160.00	
	Box (5 or more)	126.00	25	135.00	35	144.00	
	Box (20 or more)	112.00	20	120.00	0	128.00	
Filter Paper	Box	3.80	0	4.00	0	4.40	
	Case of 12 Boxes	38.00	18	40.00	20	44.00	
	Case (10 or more)	34.00	10	35.00	0	38.00	
Pasteur Pipettes	Box	3.50	0	4.00	2	4.60	
	Case of 12 Boxes	35.00	0	40.00	9	46.00	
	Case (4 or more)	32.00	10	36.00	0	41.00	
Disposable Gloves	Box	3.50	0	4.25	28	6.00	
	Case of 12 Boxes	35.00	2	42.00	0	60.00	
Methylene Chloride	4 liter bottle	16.00	0	24.00	20	36.00	
	Case of 4x4L Bots	55.00	12	80.00	7	120.00	
	1 liter bottle	7.00	0	10.00	6	14.00	
	Case of 4x1L Bots	24.00	2	32.00	2	45.00	

(continued)

TABLE 3   (continued)

Material/Supply	Unit of Measure	1988		1989		1990	
		Cost per Unit	Quantity (Units)	Cost per Unit	Quantity (Units)	Cost per Unit	Quantity (Units)
Trichlorotrifluroeth	4 liter bottle	$ 25.00	0	$ 40.00	10	$ 120.00	
	Case of 4x4L Bots	90.00	4	150.00	1	360.00	
	1 liter bottle	9.00	0	15.00	2	48.00	
	Case of 4x1L Bots	32.00	1	52.00	0	160.00	
Acetone	4 liter bottle	12.00	3	16.00	14	22.00	
	Case of 4x4L Bots	42.00	8	56.00	4	77.00	
	1 liter bottle	5.00	0	7.00	2	9.00	
	Case of 4x1L Bots	17.00	2	24.00	2	30.00	
BNA Analytical Standard	Set	1200.00	2	1500.00	1	1700.00	
VOA Analytical Standard	Set	150.00	2	200.00	1	400.00	
PEST/PCB Analytical	Set	400.00	1	500.00	0	550.00	
BNA Internal Standard	Each	12.00	12	15.00	68	20.00	
	Pack of 50	400.00	4	500.00	1	700.00	
VOA Internal Standard	Each	4.50	8	5.50	79	11.00	
	Pack of 50	180.00	2	220.00	0	440.00	
PEST/PCB Internal Standard	Each	4.00	19	5.00	47	6.00	
	Pack of 50	160.00	1	200.00	0	240.00	

Notes:

(1) Each year's data based on a 12.5% sample of invoices for purchased materials.

(2) Number of invoices sampled: for 1988 n=55; for 1989 n=73;

(3) Number of sampled invoices having expediting charges and the total expediting charges in the sample: for 1988, $273, n=5; for 1989, $1694, n=22;

(4) Data not available for 1990.

pated changes. The measures they had now certainly weren't satisfactory. At least some, perhaps most, of the information required was clearly available. "I guess my first task," he thought, "is to develop and implement the measures I need." He jotted this down on his note pad and began to make notes for other steps that he thought were necessary.

As he drove out Camelback Road toward home, John started thinking about quality at the lab. His concerns about quality were twofold. First, he was bothered that SRL did not have a Quality Assurance Officer. Many analytic protocols require that quality be assured by an individual who reports directly to the chief operating officer. This person (or others under his or her direction) are charged with a number of responsibilities, including assuring that correct analytic procedures and protocols are followed and that analyses are correct. This mandates that the quality officer prepare spikes and submit them for analysis. Spikes are samples that contain a known concentration of a specified substance. They are submitted for analysis, and the results are checked for accuracy.

For reasons of cost, SRL had not replaced the previous Quality Assurance Officer when she quit about four months ago. To their credit, the supervisors of each laboratory have been preparing spikes for analysis. They were doing this on their own initiative. Nevertheless, the supervisors all expressed worry that errors in analysis might be going undetected. Some errors had been detected, and some customer complaints had been received. The supervisors had all asked John to try to get Georgia Hoffman to hire a Quality Assurance Officer. On her own initiative, one of the supervisors, Marta Allison, had prepared a package of material related to quality assurance. Among other things, it contained a summary of the results from the supervisors' spikes (Table 4). It also contained the results of the last several PAT Rounds conducted by the Industrial Hygiene Association of America (Table 5). John made a mental note to look more carefully at these results on Monday.

He reflected on SRL's "Complaint/Quality Problem Report." Each time an error was found or a complaint was received, this form had to be completed. It required that the source of the problem be identified and recommended corrective actions be proposed. These reports were being submitted directly to Georgia Hoffman. In fact, she had designed the form herself and initiated its use. Either she or someone in Sales would contact the customer if that seemed desirable. There was a file folder full of such complaints. No systematic analysis of the causes of problems had ever been undertaken.

John took the supervisors' statements and actions as encouraging signs of an interest in quality and a commitment to improving it. He wanted to support them and, if possible, he wanted to find ways to

TABLE 4 Results of Supervisors' QA Spikes

Analyte	Date	SRL Value	Actual Value	Analyte	Date	SRL Value	Actual Value
Lead	8/88	0.00276	0.00275	Benzene	8/88	0.00239	0.00237
	10/88	0.00107	0.00110		10/88	0.00146	0.00150
	12/88	0.00181	0.00183		12/88	0.00116	0.00113
	8/14/89	0.00088	0.00083		8/22/89	0.00256	0.00251
	9/23/89	0.00310	0.00314		9/29/89	0.00071	0.00078
	10/19/89	0.00175	0.00172		10/26/89	0.00165	0.00172
	11/15/89	0.00269	0.00262		11/22/89	0.00154	0.00147
	12/14/89	0.00076	0.00079		12/18/89	0.00088	0.00093
	1/18/90	0.00159	0.00153		1/22/90	0.00198	0.00191
Arsenic	8/88	0.00130	0.00127	Toluene	8/88	0.00081	0.00077
	10/88	0.00087	0.00088		10/88	0.00185	0.00182
	12/88	0.00153	0.00155		12/88	0.00242	0.00244
	8/14/89	0.00211	0.00202		8/22/89	0.00194	0.00189
	9/23/89	0.00128	0.00118		9/29/89	0.00101	0.00094
	10/19/89	0.00068	0.00073		10/26/89	0.00237	0.00246
	11/15/89	0.00188	0.00182		11/22/89	0.00079	0.00084
	12/14/89	0.00234	0.00244		12/18/89	0.00224	0.00217
	1/18/90	0.00051	0.00058		1/22/90	0.00169	0.00179
Cadmium	8/88	0.00198	0.00202	Ethylene	8/88	0.00195	0.00190
	10/88	0.00150	0.00152		10/88	0.00223	0.00226
	12/88	0.00108	0.00105		12/88	0.00081	0.00083
	8/16/89	0.00193	0.00188		8/22/89	0.00207	0.00202
	9/24/89	0.00071	0.00075		9/29/89	0.00156	0.00148
	10/20/89	0.00272	0.00263		10/26/89	0.00090	0.00095

(continued)

TABLE 4 (continued)

Analyte	Date	SRL Value	Actual Value	Analyte	Date	SRL Value	Actual Value
	11/17/89	0.00111	0.00118		11/22/89	0.00210	0.00201
	12/14/89	0.00069	0.00074		12/18/89	0.00067	0.00072
	1/18/90	0.00166	0.00158		1/22/90	0.00152	0.00159
Chromium	8/88	0.00254	0.00250	Xylene	8/88	0.00156	0.00159
	10/88	0.00121	0.00123		10/88	0.00241	0.00244
	12/88	0.00195	0.00198		12/88	0.00078	0.00076
	8/16/89	0.00082	0.00078		8/22/89	0.00158	0.00153
	9/24/89	0.00189	0.00182		9/29/89	0.00055	0.00048
	10/20/89	0.00252	0.00249		10/26/89	0.00138	0.00133
	11/17/89	0.00079	0.00084		11/22/89	0.00282	0.00291
	12/14/89	0.00180	0.00171		12/18/89	0.00161	0.00168
	1/18/90	0.00240	0.00233		1/22/90	0.00037	0.00046

TABLE 5 Results of PAT Rounds

Round	Analyte	SRL Value	Actual Value	Number of Labs	Std Dev	Lower Limit	Upper Limit	Number Failing	Status
101	Lead	0.00150	0.00148	312	0.00002	0.00144	0.00152	16	Pass
	Mercury	0.00422	0.00418	332	0.00004	0.00410	0.00426	17	Pass
	Benzene	0.00085	0.00084	288	0.00005	0.00074	0.00094	14	Pass
	Toluene	0.00233	0.00230	276	0.00006	0.00218	0.00242	14	Pass
102	Lead	0.00287	0.00290	323	0.00003	0.00284	0.00296	16	Pass
	Cobalt	0.00128	0.00127	309	0.00003	0.00121	0.00133	15	Pass
	Benzene	0.00244	0.00248	275	0.00006	0.00236	0.00260	14	Pass
	Ethylene	0.00097	0.00096	275	0.00004	0.00088	0.00104	14	Pass
103	Lead	0.00161	0.00157	290	0.00006	0.00145	0.00169	15	Pass
	Silver	0.00298	0.00298	305	0.00005	0.00288	0.00308	15	Pass
	Xylene	0.00113	0.00111	266	0.00004	0.00103	0.00119	13	Pass
	Ethyl Benzene	0.00286	0.00288	279	0.00005	0.00278	0.00298	14	Pass
104	Arsenic	0.00043	0.00040	310	0.00005	0.00030	0.00050	16	Pass
	Barium	0.00189	0.00194	302	0.00006	0.00182	0.00206	15	Pass
	Toluene	0.00102	0.00105	289	0.00004	0.00097	0.00113	14	Pass
	Formaldehyde	0.00173	0.00174	258	0.00007	0.00160	0.00188	13	Pass
105	Lead	0.00075	0.00078	357	0.00004	0.00070	0.00086	18	Pass
	Copper	0.00368	0.00375	342	0.00005	0.00365	0.00385	17	Pass
	Benzene	0.00197	0.00190	302	0.00004	0.00182	0.00198	15	Pass
	Toluene	-0.00101	0.00107	298	0.00006	0.00095	0.00119	15	Pass
106	Lead	0.00278	0.00267	362	0.00006	0.00255	0.00279	18	Pass
	Chromium	0.00087	0.00098	352	0.00007	0.00084	0.00112	18	Pass
	Xylene	0.00255	0.00252	277	0.00005	0.00242	0.00262	14	Pass
	Methanol	0.00412	0.00406	307	0.00004	0.00398	0.00414	15	Pass

TABLE 5 (continued)

Round	Analyte	SRL Value	Actual Value	Number of Labs	Std Dev	Lower Limit	Upper Limit	Number Failing	Status
107	Arsenic	0.00132	0.00125	357	0.00005	0.00115	0.00135	18	Pass
	Mercury	0.00181	0.00188	359	0.00004	0.00180	0.00196	18	Pass
	Xylene Oxide	0.00279	0.00268	282	0.00006	0.00256	0.00280	14	Pass
	Chloroform	0.00096	0.00103	277	0.00005	0.00093	0.00113	14	Pass
108	Barium	0.00243	0.00251	337	0.00005	0.00241	0.00261	17	Pass
	Selenium	0.00102	0.00096	333	0.00004	0.00088	0.00104	17	Pass
	Benzene	0.00078	0.00084	310	0.00004	0.00076	0.00092	16	Pass
	Toluene	0.00096	0.00086	308	0.00006	0.00074	0.00098	15	Pass

Note: The Industrial Hygiene Association of America (IHAA) is a trade association that has established codes of conduct and standards of performance. It administers a certification program that is widely recognized in the industry. Many consumers of industrial hygiene services only use IHAA certified laboratories. Certification requires passing IHAA's quality testing program, Proficiency Analysis Testing (PAT), in which samples with known concentrations of selected contaminants (spikes) are sent to laboratories across the nation. Each laboratory is scored and graded in comparison to the true values and in comparison to all other participating laboratories (in other words, each lab is scored on both an absolute scale and on a curve). There are four rounds of testing each year, hence the name PAT Rounds.

build on their desire to improve quality. This brought him to his second concern about quality at the lab. There seemed to be a very narrow definition of quality and a limited view on who was responsible for assuring it and improving it. Who, he wondered, should be involved in the formulation of a broader definition of quality? What should that definition encompass? What measures of quality should be developed to support the broader definition? And, perhaps most importantly, how could he get the necessary people to buy into and participate in a total quality management concept?

CASE 2

Salt River Labs: Maintenance, Purchasing, and Materials Management

MONDAY, 7:58 AM

John Saunders arrived at his office at Salt River Labs (SRL) to begin his second week as Vice President of Production. During his first week he had met and talked with a number of the people in both the production and administrative areas of SRL. He had learned of a number of problems that seemed to be interfering with production and of a number of concerns related, not only to production, but to other areas within the company as well. John had spent a good portion of his weekend thinking about some of these problems, especially those that appeared to impact SRL's quality and productivity. He had a list of things he wanted to do, information he wanted to obtain, and people with whom he wanted to talk.

After dropping his briefcase in his office, he started down the hall to look in on the supervisors and the chemists in the laboratories. He wanted to engage in some friendly conversation with the lab people and get a sense of the atmosphere in the labs. He had discovered in his first week that there was a considerable amount of tension, even anger and hostility, toward management. There was a definite "we-they" attitude on the part of the people in the labs—and, to be honest, on the part of management. It was for this reason he had turned down the office next to all the other executives in the administrative wing of the building in favor of a smaller office out in the laboratory. One of his goals was to break down the "we-they" split and develop more of a spirit of teamwork. The other reason for making the rounds to look in on people was to ask if they had any problems with which he could help. This day he got more than he bargained for.

8:27 AM

By the time he got back to his office, John had heard about equipment failures, non-availability of chemicals and supplies, safety problems, late jobs, incorrect or incomplete work orders, and a host of other problems. He sat down to look at the list he had made while talking with the supervisors and lab personnel.

8:32 AM

Marta Allison came into John's office to tell him more about the problem with the autosampler that had stopped over the weekend. This would cause jobs to be late. Furthermore, this was not an isolated event. According to Marta it "has happened too often." She doesn't know exactly how often, or why, but the autosamplers seem to stop running frequently. This is especially annoying (and disruptive of work schedules) when the equipment fails after the chemists have gone home for the day. A chemist will set up an autosampler with 50 or more samples to be analyzed overnight. If the run aborts after only five or ten samples, the samples will have to be reloaded into the autosampler or, often, analyzed by hand. In any case, a considerable amount of time is lost.

Marta also asked about the autosampler that had been sent to Hewlett-Packard (HP) for repair. She understood it was repaired and had been ready to be returned for four months. But, despite her repeated requests and those of Dennis Farina (Manager of Industrial Hygiene), the autosampler had not been picked up. John remembered hearing about this last week and, while listening to Marta, pulled out his notes. As Marta was turning to leave, Linda Lacy came in with the WIP (work in process) report. John set the equipment problem notes aside to look at later and began to review the WIP report. He asked Marta to stay in case he had any questions.

In reviewing the WIP report, John noticed that several jobs were due out today and several others were due out last week. There were six late jobs in the Industrial Hygiene lab. Two of the late jobs were in IH–Organic and four were in IH–Inorganic. The Environmental lab also had two late jobs and no jobs were overdue in Microscopy. Marta needed to get some papers out of her office to further discuss these jobs and left to retrieve them.

8:51 AM

Marta came back into John's office and handed him her list of IH–Organic jobs that were overdue and a list of those due out today and tomorrow. On the lists she had noted their status, when they would be out, and the reason for lateness for those that were late. Marta went through the list of overdue jobs and pointed out that only one was due to problems with the analysis. On that particular job, when Marta reviewed the results of the analysis, she wasn't satisfied. She asked the chemist to redo the analysis, and she reviewed each step with him. It turned out that although his method was correct, the standard (a pre-prepared sample with a known concentration of a chemical compound) had expired and was no longer usable. Standards are purchased from a chemical supplier, and SRL did not have a current standard with which to perform this analysis. Marta had requisitioned a new standard, but wasn't sure when it would arrive.

Marta pointed out that all the other late or to-be-late jobs were also waiting for chemicals or standards required to do the analyses. One was an analysis not on the SRL price list (a catalog of the analyses performed) and required a chemical and a standard that SRL doesn't routinely stock. In fact, according to Marta, SRL had never done this analysis before and had never had this standard in house. Somewhat acidly, she pointed out that no one in sales had consulted with her (or anyone else in the lab) before selling the job and promising the due date. The chemical and the standard were requested as soon as the job arrived, and management was informed of the situation. The standard wasn't ordered for three days, wasn't shipped for four days after that, and still had not arrived. Marta was angry that the due date had not been changed and that "her people" were being blamed for this job being late. She was also angry that the customer had not been notified that the job would be late. "What kind of service is that to provide our customers?" she asked, staring at John. "Someone should have called the customer as soon as we knew it would be late, and we knew it would be late as soon as we saw what the customer was asking for."

Marta continued describing the reasons for the other late jobs, all of which needed chemicals or standards that "we should always have on hand." The materials had been requested via requisition weeks ago. She didn't know when (or if) they had actually been ordered.

9:13 AM

Jim Hoberman came into John's office to complain that "we're out of 2ml vials. Also we're just about out of methylene chloride. We need that for several jobs due out this week." According to Jim, both items had been requested two weeks ago. They had also been requested four weeks ago and six weeks earlier. He showed John photocopies of the requisitions. He keeps copies of every requisition so that he can track them to see if the supplies get ordered. "That way I have my backside covered when someone in management comes over here to blame us for not getting the job out on time. I show them the requisition and tell them that I'll get the work out if they get me the materials."

After Jim left his office, John took a few minutes to unpack his brief-case, to sort things out, to revise his "to do today" list in light of this morning's developments, and to figure out what he should do next. His first order of business was to investigate the problems brought up by Marta and Jim.

11:17 AM

With soda in hand, John returned to his office, sat down, and began to review the findings from his investigations. He made a list of what he had learned about the several requisitions that Marta and Jim had mentioned. Beyond the specifics of the particular purchase requests that he had investigated, he had learned how the purchasing of supplies and materials was handled.

When a chemist needs something (chemicals, standards, glassware, rubber gloves, and so on), the first step is to see if it can be obtained from inventory or from a chemist in one of the other laboratories. This can be frustrating and time consuming because there is no record of the inventory, there is no real order to the storage system, and many of the supplies and materials were still not unpacked from the time when they were moved from SRL's old facility. SRL moved into their current build-ing nine months ago. John heard stories of chemists spending hours looking for things without finding them only to be told later by another chemist "I saw some of that when I was looking for something last week." Of course, most of the time, the second chemist couldn't remember just where he or she had seen the buried treasure.

If the needed item cannot be located in house, the chemist gets a requisition from Susie Martinez (a microscopist in the asbestos laboratory who spends two to three half-days per week doing the purchasing). Sometimes, if Susie is out of the lab, there is a delay ranging from a few minutes to a day or two before the requisition form is obtained. After completing the requisition, which sometimes requires looking through suppliers' catalogs, the chemist gives it to his or her supervisor for approval and signature. If the supervisor is busy or out of the lab, the requisition is left in the supervisor's in box to be signed later. Since money for supplies and materials is very tightly controlled, the supervisor frequently decides the quantity to be ordered.

If the supervisor approves the request (which he or she always does unless he or she knows of some "secret stash" of the item), he or she signs the requisition, makes a photocopy for the lab file, and gives the signed requisition to Susie (or puts it in Susie's in box in the purchasing office). When Susie gets back to it, she double checks to be sure the information on the requisition (for example, item description, catalog part number, and price) is correct. Quite often Susie has to find the chemist to clarify some information or suggest a different item or vendor. According to Susie, the chemists often "don't really pay attention to the difference between two similar items" and "they usually only look in one vendor's catalog, rather than comparing the prices from other vendors." Sometimes she will ask if a smaller quantity would be acceptable. Of course, she might have to go to the supervisor to get this latter question answered. She then fills out a purchase order, assigns a number to it, records it on a list she keeps of all the purchase orders, makes a photocopy of it for her file, and takes it to Barbara Bensen in Accounting. If Barbara is not immediately available, Susie leaves the purchase order in Barbara's in basket. Finally, Susie files her copies of the requisition and the purchase order.

Barbara takes the purchase order to Arthur Gregory (Senior Vice President–Finance) for his approval. As near as John could discover, Barbara didn't actually do anything with the purchase order except deliver it to Arthur. The reason it went to her was, in Arthur's words, "so she'll know about it." So, she knows about the "requested" purchase order, but she doesn't make any encumbrances or record the information anywhere. John noted that the purchase order had not yet been approved at this stage and, apparently, many of them never do get approved.

In a lot of ways, John thought to himself, his conversation with Arthur had been the most enlightening. Arthur has mandated that he personally approve every purchase order, and he doesn't do so until he's "convinced that we really need the item." One thing Arthur firmly believes is that "chemists don't even think about costs. They just order whatever they think they may need without checking to see if we already have it." Arthur had continued, "We don't even know what we have. I don't approve *anything* until they convince me that they have looked to see if we already have it."

Arthur made it clear that he is "trying to control costs and manage cash flows" because "the cash flow situation is so tight." He confirmed what John had learned earlier from other sources, that the company did have a severe cash flow problem and considerable debts. "We have a very difficult situation. Someone has to make the decisions about which bills to pay and which items to order. The chemists just don't understand. They don't think in terms of costs and cash flow. I ask them to prioritize their requests, but they always put everything as 'high priority.' You know that just can't be. Not *everything* can be high priority. I simply don't believe them."

Arthur seldom "disapproves" a purchase order; he simply doesn't approve it "at this time"—his idea being that he will "allocate the funds" and only approve those that are "of highest priority." He presumes that the unapproved requests will be resubmitted when they have "a higher priority." John observed (to himself) that the items on which the lab was now out of stock (and, consequently, missing customer due dates) had all been "not approved" at least once.

If Arthur does not approve and sign the purchase order, he gives it back to Barbara who gives it back to Susie. Susie simply puts it in a folder she keeps that contains the "awaiting approval" (as she calls them) purchase orders and resubmits it later. Sometimes she seeks out the chemist or supervisor to let them know the status, but usually she doesn't. She waits until they come to ask her about it. "Otherwise, I'd be looking for them all the time since most POs don't get approved the first time."

If Arthur does approve the purchase order, he gives it to Barbara, who gives it to Susie. At this point, John thought, the process became a little unclear. Sometimes, but not often, Susie goes ahead and places the order. This, it seems, occurred most often when she was dealing with a new vendor to whom SRL didn't owe money. More often, she gave the purchase order to Paul Jensen, the Controller, who called the vendor and negotiated to get the order filled.

From his brief discussion with Paul, John had learned how bad the situation really was. "Most vendors won't ship to us except COD, or if we wire a cash transfer, or they have a certified check in their hands. Some won't do business at all because we owe them money. Several (he wouldn't reveal the exact number) have judgments against us. They have been lied to too many times." Paul, it turned out, had been hired just two months ago, primarily to deal with SRL's creditors. Since then he has been trying to negotiate arrangements that "will let us get the materials we need to do business. I try to explain to them that it's not in their interest for us to go under."

Paul had explained that three major suppliers have agreed to fill orders if they receive a certified cashier's check for twice the amount of the order. Half the amount was applied to the current order, the other half was applied to existing debt. He wasn't sure if this debt payment was showing up as current materials cost in financial reports (he thought it was) or as debt repayment. This arrangement worked pretty well, but money was so tight that Arthur kept pushing to "find new vendors" who would accept orders on credit. Paul explained that SRL was "running out of vendors. We owe money to just about all of them."

Currently, SRL is using a local middleman distributor to get some supplies and materials, especially chemicals, at a price about 20–30% above the cost of buying direct from the manufacturer. They are also buying through Georgia Hoffman's brother's company in Seattle. This delayed the receipt of much needed items because the goods were transshipped. They weren't shipped directly to SRL so that the vendors wouldn't recognize the address. This also added steps and time to the purchase process.

After talking with Arthur and Paul, John had gone to talk with Jim, Marta, and Dennis. Jim and Marta had estimated that they each spend up to an hour each day trying to get supplies ordered and received. Jim said that "Susie spends most of her time, more than the two half-days she's supposed to be spending on purchasing, filling out POs, discussing them with Arthur, calling to get prices and finding out who will sell to us, and following up two, three, four times with Arthur to get a PO released." Dennis continued, "We never get quantity discounts. We usually end up paying Federal Express, air freight costs, or other expediting premiums because we issue the POs so late. And even then, we still get things late."

Following his discussion with Jim, Marta, and Dennis, John had returned to his office to think about everything he had learned and to get out his notes from his meetings last week when some of the same complaints had surfaced. It was clear to him that getting SRL to run the way it should would be a much bigger chore than he had realized. He looked at his watch, 12:10, time for lunch. But first, he picked up his phone and called Georgia Hoffman. She wasn't in, but was expected back at about 1:00.

1:46 PM

John was back in his office running over in his mind his conversation with Georgia Hoffman. He had gone to talk with her as soon as he had gotten back from lunch. He had raised the issue of autosamplers, especially the one at HP. The gist of her response was "we can't afford to buy or lease any additional autosamplers. Nor can we afford to pay for and pick up the one that is at HP." Further, Georgia does not want to have a maintenance/service contract. She doesn't believe they are worthwhile.

As he reflected on her comments, and her manner while making them, he concluded that he didn't believe her. He thought she just didn't want to spend the money. However, she was willing to let him retrieve the autosampler from HP if he could talk them into giving it to him.

At this point, Marta came in to inform him that "one of the two autosamplers that we do have has malfunctioned several times today; not the one that stopped over the weekend, the other one. Three jobs that were scheduled for completion today so that they could be typed and mailed 'on-time' tomorrow will not get done today." She continued by telling him that they *may* be able to get them done by tomorrow "if somebody is willing to stay tonight" to do the work by hand. "It will require someone staying until about midnight and then coming back in at 8:00 in the morning to interpret and write up the results."

John talked with Marta about the immediate problem, and they agreed she would try to find a chemist to stay and run the analysis. John suggested a second chemist might be able to finish the analysis tomorrow morning, as long as he was involved this afternoon. After she left, he made some notes about everything that had happened, his discussion with Marta, and some ideas of things he wanted to think about and/or do regarding these various issues. Then (finally!) he looked at the list he had made up over the weekend of things he wanted to do today and this week.

WEDNESDAY

It was late in the afternoon, early evening really. John leaned back in his chair and reflected how this seemed to be the only time he really had to do anything that required contemplation, writing, or just sitting and analyzing information. Until nearly everyone else had gone home for the day, he was simply buried under a barrage of problems needing solution and requests for help and/or information. He began looking over the notes and information he had gathered in the last two days. He was astonished at some of what he had found. On Monday he had gotten a brief picture of how the requisition and purchasing process operated. Further investigation yesterday and today had confirmed that his initial understanding was accurate. He had further learned that the "files" on purchasing were very informal and not well organized. The old requisitions and purchase orders were simply kept in a few folders, more or less in chronological order. Susie numbered the POs by hand when she completed them. She kept them in one folder until the orders were actually placed. Then she moved them to another "open order" folder until the order was received. Once the order was received, she moved the PO to a "closed" folder.

John had reviewed a sample of the POs, recording the dates when the requisition leading to the PO was completed, when the PO was filled out, when the order was actually placed, and how long it had taken to receive the material ordered. In some cases, the process was very quick, with the PO being issued the same day as the requisition and the material being received by expedited delivery the next day or the day after. In some cases, although the PO was written and dated within a day of the requisition, there was a delay of as much as a month or more before the issuance of the PO (after which the material was shipped on an expedited basis for an extra charge). In some cases, two or three requisitions dated anywhere from a week to a month or more apart were stapled together and covered by a single PO. Usually the one PO was for the same amount as just one of the requests (rather than for the total). He also pulled out all the POs issued during the last 12 months for a selected sample of items. He learned that all items were treated essentially the same as far as purchasing went. No more attention, no less attention, was paid to any particular item. All the POs had Arthur Gregory's signature on them.

The other surprising discovery was that there were no inventory records at all. Material that was received was given to the person ordering it. No one knew how much of anything was on hand in the laboratories. There really were some materials and supplies in boxes in the basement not yet unpacked from the move. No one knew what was in those boxes, or how much of it there was.

He knew he would have to develop purchasing and inventory systems. He knew that to do this "right" would take considerable time.

"What, if anything," he wondered, "can I do right now? We need something quick, simple, inexpensive, easy to implement, and easy to use. And yet it has to give us some control over materials and some information to manage the materials functions."

After an hour or so working on this problem, he packed up his briefcase and headed for home. "I'll work on this more tonight and have some kind of plan ready for tomorrow."

CASE 3

Salt River Labs: Strategy, Forecasting, and Capacity

As he left the weekly Executive Staff Committee meeting, John Saunders was pleased, concerned, and a little puzzled. He had been attending these meetings since he started as Vice President of Production at Salt River Labs back at the beginning of February. Now, in the first week of July, Georgia Hoffman, the President and owner of SRL, had announced her Strategic Plan for the next five years. John was pleased for two reasons. This was, after all, the first time consideration of strategy issues had been the focus of the weekly Executive Staff Committee meeting. He was also pleased to see that the final numbers for June had confirmed a trend toward profitability. What puzzled and concerned John was the manner in which strategy had been introduced into the meeting, the actions Georgia had taken, and the content of the Strategic Plan.

Previously, the weekly Monday morning meetings had focused exclusively on what had happened during the previous week and on what was going to happen during the current week. This had certainly seemed appropriate back in February when SRL had just finished posting its eighteenth straight month of losses, had trouble getting work out on time, had trouble getting supplies from vendors, and had trouble meeting its biweekly payroll. As the picture improved during the next few months, John and some of the others on the executive committee had urged that they begin thinking strategically about the next 12 to 24 months, and even about the next five years.

Most of those in attendance at this week's meeting (see Figure 1) had no idea that strategy would even be an item on the agenda. They had

Figure 1   *Salt River Labs Organizational Chart*

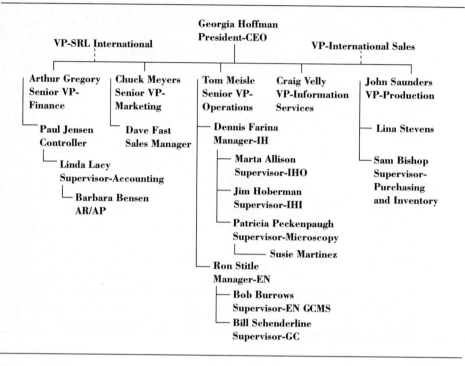

not been consulted at all on this topic. Instead, Georgia had announced her Strategic Plan to expand from SRL's one location doing about $2.5 million of sales to "20 laboratories doing $50 million in sales" in the next five years. It became apparent during the ensuing discussion that Arthur Gregory, the Senior Vice President–Finance, was the only one with whom Georgia had really discussed this. She said that she was in the process of lining up venture capital money to pay off SRL's $2 million debt and finance the beginning of the expansion. She also announced that she had hired two new Vice Presidents, one to head SRL International and one to manage International Sales. She then asked everyone else to draw up plans for their areas to accomplish the expansion.

On his way back to his office, John stopped off at Lina Stevens's office. As John's assistant, Lina had already done a variety of projects since being hired two months earlier. These projects mostly involved generating information for planning or evaluating the ideas that John had for improving SRL's production operations. As he sat down in

Lina's office, John explained what had just occurred in the executive committee meeting. After he and Lina discussed the situation for a few minutes, John walked down the hall to ask Dennis Farina (Manager of Industrial Hygiene) and Ron Stitle (Manager of the Environmental laboratory) to join them. He knew Patricia Peckenpaugh (Supervisor of Microscopy) was out of the office and made a mental note to catch her as soon as she returned.

As the four of them discussed this new development, they began to generate numerous ideas about tasks that should be undertaken and information that should be collected in order to prepare a response to Georgia's request. After the others left Lina's office, John turned to her and asked, "Lina, do you think you could prepare some forecasts for us?" After she indicated her willingness to do so, she asked John just what he wanted. "Well," he said as he picked up a marker and started making notes on the white board on the wall, "we'd better try to get some projection of the demand for the next 12 months, the next 24 months, and the next five years. Use whatever level of aggregation you think is appropriate." After a pause he added, "... and most useful."

"Also, you'd better include a variety of scenarios of growth. Maybe you can include one scenario that reflects our current trends, a second one that has us keeping up with the market plus picking up a few percentage points in our market share, and a third that's based on growth that will fulfill Georgia's plans."

They talked a bit more about the specifics of the forecasts Lina was going to prepare. Lina asked if SRL's income statements (Table 1) would be a good source of data. John replied, "Yes, and so might that table I got from Craig Velly (Vice President–Information Services) with the figures on the number of analyses performed (Table 2). It also has data on how prices have changed over the last three years. Do the best you can with what's available. Then, if there's anything else you think would be helpful, or anything you need, ask. If you can't get it, let me know and I'll see if I can get it for you. Use your own discretion about how you structure the forecasting models and about what information you need."

As John was about to leave her office, Lina asked, "What about turning the demand forecasts into capacity requirements? Not that I don't have enough to do, but, if I don't ask now, you'll be back down here in ten minutes going, 'Oh yeah, I forgot to ask ... ' and asking me to do that."

John smiled somewhat sheepishly. "You're right," he said, "and while you're at it, you had better consider both labor and equipment. You have a copy of that utilization report you did for me, don't you? (Table 3)" Lina nodded. "And the labor hour/labor cost report? (Table 4)" Lina nodded

TABLE 1 Income Statement 1990

	JAN	FEB	MAR	APR	MAY	JUN
GROSS PROFIT MARGINS						
MICROSCOPY						
Sales Revenues	26,068	42,207	48,658	73,207	82,330	76,000
Cost of Sales	23,915	21,820	25,834	26,580	27,331	26,019
Gross Profit	2,153	20,387	22,824	46,627	54,999	49,981
Gross Profit Margin	8.3%	48.3%	46.9%	63.7%	66.8%	65.8%
INDUSTRIAL HYGIENE						
Sales Revenues	100,308	140,248	126,207	108,928	114,370	117,622
Cost of Sales	42,525	42,139	38,313	36,209	37,205	36,187
Gross Profit	57,783	98,109	87,894	72,719	77,165	81,435
Gross Profit Margin	57.6%	70.0%	69.6%	66.8%	67.5%	69.2%
ENVIRONMENTAL						
Sales Revenues	23,392	26,729	44,765	74,529	38,948	55,729
Cost of Sales	26,543	22,906	28,347	34,777	27,991	31,664
Gross Profit	(3,151)	3,823	16,418	39,752	10,957	24,065
Gross Profit Margin	-13.5%	14.3%	36.7%	53.3%	28.1%	43.2%
LABORATORY TOTAL						
Sales Revenues	149,768	209,184	219,630	256,664	235,648	249,351
Cost of Sales	92,983	86,865	92,494	97,566	92,527	93,870
Gross Profit	56,785	122,319	127,136	159,098	143,121	155,481
Gross Profit Margin	37.9%	58.5%	57.9%	62.0%	60.7%	62.4%
NON–LABORATORY OTHER						
Sales Revenues	3,753	9,335	7,082	4,401	14,859	7,220
Cost of Sales	7,643	8,274	7,743	7,420	7,688	7,531
Gross Profit	(3,890)	1,061	(661)	(3,019)	7,171	(311)
Gross Profit Margin	-103.7%	11.4%	-9.3%	-68.6%	48.3%	-4.3%
LAB+NONLAB TOTAL						
Sales Revenues	153,521	218,519	226,712	261,065	250,507	250,571
Cost of Sales	100,626	95,139	100,237	104,986	100,215	101,401
Gross Profit	52,895	123,380	126,475	156,079	150,292	155,170
Gross Profit Margin	34.5%	56.5%	55.8%	59.8%	60.0%	60.5%

(continued)

TABLE 1 (continued) 1990

	JAN	FEB	MAR	APR	MAY	JUN
OPERATING EXPENSES						
Customer Service	12,874	11,755	10,902	10,231	9,878	9,573
Sales/Marketing	17,794	16,498	15,967	19,925	26,166	23,856
General & Admin.	66,500	72,111	78,266	83,575	89,861	81,515
Depreciation	1,651	1,651	1,651	1,651	1,651	1,651
Bad Debt Expense	0	0	0	0	0	0
Repairs & Maint.	0	2,500	1,500	875	450	900
Total	98,819	104,515	108,286	116,257	128,006	117,495
PROFIT (LOSS) BEFORE INTEREST & TAXES	(45,924)	18,865	18,189	39,822	22,286	37,675
OTHER INCOME/EXPENSE						
Interest Income/Exp	(13,477)	(13,378)	(15,886)	(13,351)	(13,762)	(13,500)
Miscellaneous						
Total	(13,477)	(13,378)	(15,886)	(13,351)	(13,762)	(13,500)
NET INCOME (LOSS) BEFORE TAXES	(59,401)	5,487	2,303	26,471	8,524	24,175

(continued)

TABLE 1 (continued) **Income Statement 1989**

	JAN	FEB	MAR	APR	MAY	JUN	JUL	AUG	SEP	OCT	NOV	DEC	TOTAL
GROSS PROFIT MARGINS													
MICROSCOPY													
Sales Revenues	69,134	50,734	51,938	48,127	38,994	44,082	30,921	49,117	24,265	28,889	16,084	30,741	483,026
Cost of Sales	16,660	14,600	16,730	14,885	16,902	16,612	15,880	16,799	15,244	15,057	14,019	15,308	188,696
Gross Profit	52,474	36,134	35,208	33,242	22,092	27,470	15,041	32,318	9,021	13,832	2,065	15,433	294,330
Gross Profit Margin	75.9%	71.2%	67.8%	69.1%	56.7%	62.3%	48.6%	65.8%	37.2%	47.9%	12.8%	50.2%	60.9%
INDUSTRIAL HYGIENE													
Sales Revenues	55,531	56,907	75,950	63,841	87,984	107,778	77,380	88,911	122,238	92,588	87,531	74,446	991,085
Cost of Sales	36,191	36,784	38,102	26,937	31,587	31,669	31,929	33,490	37,453	36,366	37,216	32,491	410,215
Gross Profit	19,340	20,123	37,848	36,904	56,397	76,109	45,451	55,421	84,785	56,222	50,315	41,955	580,870
Gross Profit Margin	34.8%	35.4%	49.8%	57.8%	64.1%	70.6%	58.7%	62.3%	69.4%	60.7%	57.5%	56.4%	58.6%
ENVIRONMENTAL													
Sales Revenues	30,825	19,373	28,020	29,692	32,313	14,391	9,282	15,285	16,814	20,100	24,280	58,039	298,414
Cost of Sales	42,643	43,758	45,706	27,569	27,250	21,168	22,709	19,475	21,673	25,484	29,152	22,719	349,306
Gross Profit	(11,818)	(24,385)	(17,686)	2,123	5,063	(6,777)	(13,427)	(4,190)	(4,859)	(5,384)	(4,872)	35,320	(50,892)
Gross Profit Margin	-38.3%	-125.9%	-63.1%	7.2%	15.7%	-47.1%	-144.7%	-27.4%	-28.9%	-26.8%	-20.1%	60.9%	-17.1%
LABORATORY TOTAL													
Sales Revenues	155,490	127,014	155,908	141,660	159,291	166,251	117,583	153,313	163,317	141,577	127,895	163,226	1,772,525
Cost of Sales	95,494	95,142	100,538	69,391	75,739	69,449	70,518	69,764	74,370	76,907	80,387	70,518	948,217
Gross Profit	59,996	31,872	55,370	72,269	83,552	96,802	47,065	83,549	88,947	64,670	47,508	92,708	824,308
Gross Profit Margin	38.6%	25.1%	35.5%	51.0%	52.5%	58.2%	40.0%	54.5%	54.5%	45.7%	37.1%	56.8%	46.5%
NON-LABORATORY OTHER													
Sales Revenues	9,554	9,076	12,835	15,040	18,697	12,030	8,375	699	1,316	9,153	2,222	2,001	100,998
Cost of Sales	22,532	12,123	18,617	17,314	20,370	21,013	17,892	19,268	19,479	18,610	21,053	18,954	227,225
Gross Profit	(12,978)	(3,047)	(5,782)	(2,274)	(1,673)	(8,983)	(9,517)	(18,569)	(18,163)	(9,457)	(18,831)	(16,953)	(126,227)
Gross Profit Margin	-135.8%	-33.6%	-45.0%	-15.1%	-8.9%	-74.7%	-113.6%	-2656.5%	-1380.2%	-103.3%	-847.5%	-847.2%	-125.0%
LAB+NONLAB TOTAL													
Sales Revenues	165,044	136,090	168,743	156,700	177,988	178,281	125,958	154,012	164,633	150,730	130,117	165,227	1,873,523
Cost of Sales	118,026	107,265	119,155	86,705	96,109	90,462	88,410	89,032	93,849	95,517	101,440	89,472	1,175,442
Gross Profit	47,018	28,825	49,588	69,995	81,879	87,819	37,548	64,980	70,784	55,213	28,677	75,755	698,081
Gross Profit Margin	28.5%	21.2%	29.4%	44.7%	46.0%	49.3%	29.8%	42.2%	43.0%	36.6%	22.0%	45.8%	37.3%

(continued)

TABLE 1 (continued) 1989

	JAN	FEB	MAR	APR	MAY	JUN	JUL	AUG	SEP	OCT	NOV	DEC	TOTAL
OPERATING EXPENSES													
Customer Service	15,967	15,531	20,961	13,466	13,053	12,123	11,953	9,872	9,861	10,991	11,185	12,000	156,963
Sales/Marketing	31,349	40,500	41,757	9,405	13,142	16,504	12,424	14,188	11,439	21,122	15,571	20,000	247,401
General & Admin.	90,159	67,431	83,960	65,956	74,696	66,773	120,189	85,655	78,837	82,287	81,448	82,400	979,791
Depreciation	1,701	1,701	1,701	1,701	1,701	1,701	1,701	1,651	1,651	1,651	1,651	1,651	20,162
Bad Debt Expense	500	500	500	500	500	500	500	500	1,922	500	500	500	7,422
Repairs & Maint.													0
Total	139,676	125,663	148,879	91,028	103,092	97,601	146,767	111,866	103,710	116,551	110,355	116,551	1,411,739
PROFIT (LOSS) BEFORE INTEREST & TAXES	(92,658)	(96,838)	(99,291)	(21,033)	(21,213)	(9,782)	(109,219)	(46,886)	(32,926)	(61,338)	(81,678)	(40,796)	(713,658)
OTHER INCOME/EXPENSE													
Interest Income/Exp	(14,970)	(17,981)	(11,457)	(11,016)	(11,031)	(11,045)	(36,039)	(19,631)	(18,785)	(17,330)	(17,231)	(18,000)	(204,516)
Miscellaneous	(8,176)	(381)	9	(1,686)	(290)	(880)	(244,389)	(511)	(6,209)	1,030			(261,483)
Total	(23,146)	(18,362)	(11,448)	(12,702)	(11,321)	(11,925)	(280,428)	(20,142)	(24,994)	(16,300)	(17,231)	(18,000)	(465,999)
NET INCOME (LOSS) BEFORE TAXES	(115,804)	(115,200)	(110,739)	(33,735)	(32,534)	(21,707)	(389,647)	(67,028)	(57,920)	(77,638)	(98,909)	(58,796)	(1,179,657)

(continued)

169

TABLE 1 (continued) Income Statement 1988

	JAN	FEB	MAR	APR	MAY	JUN	JUL	AUG	SEP	OCT	NOV	DEC	TOTAL
GROSS PROFIT MARGINS													
MICROSCOPY													
Sales Revenues	62,788	49,561	59,569	57,048	56,981	58,697	40,274	46,806	49,949	38,788	32,834	42,661	595,957
Cost of Sales	15,840	13,800	16,135	14,322	15,483	15,891	15,101	15,327	15,579	15,033	14,946	15,128	182,585
Gross Profit	46,948	35,761	43,434	42,726	41,498	42,806	25,173	31,479	34,370	23,755	17,888	27,533	413,372
Gross Profit Margin	74.8%	72.2%	72.9%	74.9%	72.8%	72.9%	62.5%	67.3%	68.8%	61.2%	54.5%	64.5%	69.4%
INDUSTRIAL HYGIENE													
Sales Revenues	157,269	128,965	152,348	136,720	145,541	140,670	96,519	112,173	112,913	85,768	69,103	90,256	1,428,246
Cost of Sales	36,296	35,352	36,188	35,777	34,680	34,481	32,017	33,589	34,803	34,106	36,558	37,279	421,126
Gross Profit	120,973	93,613	116,160	100,943	110,861	106,189	64,502	78,584	78,110	51,662	32,545	52,977	1,007,120
Gross Profit Margin	76.9%	72.6%	76.2%	73.8%	76.2%	75.5%	66.8%	70.1%	69.2%	60.2%	47.1%	58.7%	70.5%
ENVIRONMENTAL													
Sales Revenues	57,437	46,597	60,356	50,575	62,948	52,036	35,704	41,495	42,508	28,727	21,562	28,387	528,334
Cost of Sales	40,104	40,001	44,312	43,119	45,271	43,375	41,953	42,238	41,850	40,782	40,052	40,791	503,848
Gross Profit	17,333	6,596	16,044	7,456	17,677	8,661	(6,249)	(743)	658	(12,055)	(18,490)	(12,404)	24,486
Gross Profit Margin	30.2%	14.2%	26.6%	14.7%	28.1%	16.6%	-17.5%	-1.8%	1.5%	-42.0%	-85.7%	-43.7%	4.6%
LABORATORY TOTAL													
Sales Revenues	277,495	225,123	272,274	244,343	265,471	251,404	172,496	200,474	205,370	153,283	123,499	161,305	2,552,536
Cost of Sales	92,240	89,153	96,635	93,218	95,434	93,747	89,071	91,154	92,232	89,921	91,556	93,198	1,107,559
Gross Profit	185,255	135,970	175,639	151,125	170,037	157,657	83,425	109,320	113,138	63,362	31,943	68,107	1,444,977
Gross Profit Margin	66.8%	60.4%	64.5%	61.8%	64.1%	62.7%	48.4%	54.5%	55.1%	41.3%	25.9%	42.2%	56.6%
NON-LABORATORY OTHER													
Sales Revenues	10,481	8,503	10,284	9,229	10,027	9,495	6,515	7,572	7,757	5,789	4,665	6,092	96,409
Cost of Sales	14,877	13,661	14,222	14,748	17,590	18,128	19,810	19,533	17,107	17,599	17,841	18,549	203,665
Gross Profit	(4,396)	(5,158)	(3,938)	(5,519)	(7,563)	(8,633)	(13,295)	(11,961)	(9,350)	(11,810)	(13,176)	(12,457)	(107,256)
Gross Profit Margin	-41.9%	-60.7%	-38.3%	-59.8%	-75.4%	-90.9%	-204.1%	-158.0%	-120.5%	-204.0%	-282.5%	-204.5%	-111.3%
LAB+NONLAB TOTAL													
Sales Revenues	287,975	233,625	282,557	253,572	275,497	260,899	179,012	208,046	213,127	159,072	128,164	167,397	2,648,945
Cost of Sales	107,117	102,814	110,857	107,966	113,024	111,875	108,881	110,687	109,339	107,520	109,397	111,747	1,311,224
Gross Profit	180,858	130,811	171,700	145,606	162,473	149,024	70,131	97,359	103,788	51,552	18,767	55,650	1,337,721
Gross Profit Margin	62.8%	56.0%	60.8%	57.4%	59.0%	57.1%	39.2%	46.8%	48.7%	32.4%	14.6%	33.2%	50.5%

(continued)

TABLE 1 (continued) 1988

	JAN	FEB	MAR	APR	MAY	JUN	JUL	AUG	SEP	OCT	NOV	DEC	TOTAL
OPERATING EXPENSES													
Customer Service	15,009	15,686	16,978	12,927	13,575	13,457	11,714	10,366	11,340	13,739	14,205	15,120	164,116
Sales/Marketing	20,347	33,593	32,774	28,100	29,798	31,921	36,824	38,507	34,943	35,221	31,290	33,726	387,044
General & Admin.	60,828	55,771	64,489	68,822	74,969	67,737	76,808	82,736	78,378	84,277	84,251	82,005	881,071
Depreciation	1,811	1,811	1,811	1,811	1,811	1,701	1,701	1,651	1,651	1,651	1,651	1,651	20,712
Bad Debt Expense	875	875	875	875	875	875	875	500	500	500	500	1,350	9,475
Repairs & Maint.	925	1,058	750	750	1,275	750	750	1,000	750	0	0	0	8,008
Total	99,795	108,794	117,677	113,285	122,303	116,441	128,672	134,760	127,562	135,388	131,897	133,852	1,470,426
PROFIT (LOSS) BEFORE INTEREST & TAXES	81,063	22,017	54,023	32,320	40,170	32,583	(58,541)	(37,400)	(23,774)	(83,835)	(113,130)	(78,202)	(132,705)
OTHER INCOME/EXPENSE													
Interest Income/Exp	(9,825)	(9,825)	(11,016)	(11,016)	(10,888)	(10,982)	(12,200)	(12,321)	(13,555)	(13,780)	14,290	14,622	(86,496)
Miscellaneous	3,451	(679)	1,274	(42)	(873)	1,667	(42,586)	(737)	(8,339)	1,223	(486)	(2,306)	(48,433)
Total	(6,374)	(10,504)	(9,742)	(11,058)	(11,761)	(9,315)	(54,786)	(13,058)	(21,894)	(12,557)	13,804	12,316	(134,929)
NET INCOME (LOSS) BEFORE TAXES	74,689	11,513	44,281	21,262	28,409	23,268	(113,327)	(50,458)	(45,668)	(96,392)	(99,326)	(65,886)	(267,634)

TABLE 2 List Price, Sales Volume & Revenues for Most Common Analyses

Analyte/Analysis:	1988			1989			1990 (Jan–Jun)		
	List Price	Quantity Sold	Actual Revenue	List Price	Quantity Sold	Actual Revenue	List Price	Quantity Sold	Actual Revenue
Microscopy									
Filters	$30	13,182	$369,868	$25	13,287	$302,279	$17	9,487	$148,382
Bulk	50	4,837	226,089	40	5,020	180,746	35	6,352	200,088
Total			595,957			483,026			348,470
Industrial Hygiene (Filters,Plugs,Tubes)									
Arsenic (As)	30	2,144	60,461	25	1,523	35,410	20	1,635	30,738
Barium (Ba)	15	89	1,255	12	55	601	10	81	761
Cadmium (Cd)	15	373	5,282	12	203	2,273	10	211	1,992
Chromium (Cr)	15	2,437	33,704	12	1,562	17,563	10	1,383	12,751
Lead (Pb)	15	374	5,610	12	212	2,493	10	212	2,120
Mercury (Hg)	30	69	2,043	25	59	1,375	20	82	1,619
Selenium (Se)	30	296	8,525	25	226	5,085	20	198	3,802
Silver (Ag)	15	87	1,274	12	19	215	10	67	654
Silica (Si)	15	1,339	19,683	12	1,132	13,122	10	1,056	10,349
Benzene	30	1,433	42,431	25	1,058	25,551	20	1,137	22,285
Toluene	30	1,297	38,599	25	1,003	24,373	20	71	1,392
Ethylene	30	923	27,053	25	927	22,688	20	720	14,112
Ethyl Benzene	30	861	25,107	25	562	13,109	20	598	11,721
Xylene	30	774	22,941	25	570	13,495	20	643	12,603
BTEX	90	928	77,924	75	877	64,131	65	821	52,298
Ethylene Oxide	30	884	25,539	25	620	14,694	20	511	10,016

(continued)

TABLE 2 (continued)

Analyte/Analysis:	1988			1989			1990 (Jan-Jun)		
	List Price	Quantity Sold	Actual Revenue	List Price	Quantity Sold	Actual Revenue	List Price	Quantity Sold	Actual Revenue
Chloroform	$ 30	720	$ 21,168	$ 25	631	$ 14,371	$ 20	529	$ 10,368
Methyl Chloroform	30	659	19,553	25	667	16,075	20	544	10,662
Methylene Chloride	30	597	17,498	25	429	10,628	20	501	9,820
Methanol	30	517	15,308	25	463	11,193	20	385	7,546
Isopropyl Alcohol	30	427	12,708	25	387	8,978	20	361	7,076
Formaldehyde	30	538	15,026	25	417	10,102	20	286	5,606
Herbicides	250	52	11,895	200	40	7,632	200	73	13,009
Pesticides/PCBs	200	2,081	388,731	150	1,811	247,473	125	1,492	174,191
GC/MS Screen for Organics	300	480	134,352	250	398	90,446	200	520	97,032
Semivolatile Organics by GC/MS	400	51	18,013	300	35	9,513	300	94	24,901
Volatile Organics by GC/FID	100	3,427	328,307	85	2,891	233,694	75	1,586	113,954
Volatile Organics by GC/MS	250	83	18,260	175	49	7,863	175	39	6,006
Total			$1,398,248			$924,145			$669,381
Environmental Samples (Soil/Water)									
Arsenic (As)	$ 35	137	$ 4,651	$ 30	100	$ 3,000	$ 25	115	$2,789
Barium (Ba)	15	0	0	12	0	0	12	12	137
BTEX	125	914	111,165	90	622	45,344	65	443	27,385
Cadmium (Cd)	15	0	0	12	0	0	12	12	137

(continued)

173

TABLE 2 (continued)

Analyte/Analysis:	1988			1989			1990 (Jan-Jun)		
	List Price	Quantity Sold	Actual Revenue	List Price	Quantity Sold	Actual Revenue	List Price	Quantity Sold	Actual Revenue
Chloride	$ 15	251	$ 3,716	$ 15	197	$ 2,819	$ 15	182	$ 2,695
Chromium (Cr)	15	125	1,787	12	43	516	12	67	766
Cyanide	35	112	3,755	30	84	2,948	25	92	2,203
GC/MS Screen for Organics	400	98	37,946	300	77	20,790	250	86	20,812
Herbicides	250	257	61,250	225	192	38,491	200	155	29,552
Lead (Pb)	15	255	3,668	12	84	1,008	12	93	1,070
Mercury (Hg)	35	118	4,014	30	61	1,701	25	84	2,041
Nitrate/Nitrite	15	183	2,652	15	222	3,230	15	211	3,057
Pesticides/PCBs	200	419	77,264	150	277	39,597	150	256	35,405
pH	10	771	7,325	8	513	4,051	8	689	5,236
RCRA-8 (Ag,As,Ba,Cd, Cr,Hg,Pb,Se)	250	292	68,109	220	213	40,909	190	249	44,140
Selenium	35	97	3,225	30	66	1,913	25	103	2,446
Semivolatile Organics by GC/MS	400	128	46,848	300	103	28,768	300	86	23,607
Silica (Si)	15	282	4,230	12	88	1,056	12	149	1,788
Silver (Ag)	15	23	345	12	23	276	12	17	204
Total Petroleum Hydrocarbons	60	587	32,015	50	353	15,303	35	302	9,608
Volatile Organics by GC/MS	250	190	43,273	175	241	39,223	175	208	33,160
Total			$517,237			$290,942			$248,240

TABLE 3 Major Equipment Utilization Report

	Number of Days Observed	Number of Stoppages	7 AM to 5 PM				5 PM to 7 AM		
			Hours Running	Hours Idle	Hours Planned Maintenance	Hours Downtime (Stopped)	Hours Planned Runtime	Hours Actually Running	Hours Lost (Stopped)
Gas Chromatographs									
IH - Organic									
a. HP 5730 (with autosampler)	10	42	52	17	2	29	62	32	30
b. HP 5730 (with autosampler)	10	57	51	27	0	22	78	36	42
c. HP 5890	10	21	59	33	0	8	22	17	5
d. HP 5890	10	15	68	26	0	6	36	28	8
IH - Inorganics									
a. HP 5730	10	2	42	37	4	17	19	17	2
EN - GC									
a. HP 5890	10	0	51	47	2	0	14	14	0
b. HP 5730	10	3	38	56	0	6	4	2	2
c. Tracor 540	10	2	33	62	0	5	7	6	1
d. Varian 3400 (with autosampler)	10	3	45	48	0	7	0	0	0
EN - GC/MS									
a. HP 5890	10	2	44	47	4	5	9	7	2
b. HP 5890	10	3	51	38	4	7	2	2	0
Atomic Absorption Spectrophotometers									
a. Perkin Elmer 603	10	1	67	32	0	1	17	15	2
b. Perkin Elmer 107	10	4	72	21	0	7	23	12	11
Microscopes									
a. Zeiss (2 units)	10	0							
b. Leitz Ortholux II	10	0							
c. Weld	10	0							
d. American Optical (3 units)	10	0							
e. Stereoscope	10	0							

TABLE 4 Labor-Hours & Labor Costs by Laboratory

Semi-Monthly Period		Jan-1	Jan-2	Feb-1	Feb-2	Mar-1	Mar-2	Apr-1	Apr-2	May-1	May-2	Jun-1	Jun-2
Microscopy													
Labor Hours	Regular	603	693	585	590	640	650	637	682	672	658	647	662
	Overtime	0	0	0	0	40	72	56	83	72	108	43	65
Labor Cost	Regular	7791	8988	7634	7711	8397	8535	8377	8989	8877	8699	8573	8785
	Overtime	0	0	0	0	777	1418	1096	1648	1422	2134	864	1298
Industrial Hygiene													
Labor Hours	Regular	678	698	660	664	668	696	712	733	692	697	680	720
	Overtime	34	51	29	43	31	86	33	74	16	104	32	74
Labor Cost	Regular	10326	10645	10072	10166	10240	10691	10951	11303	10684	10790	10547	11182
	Overtime	769	1155	653	982	709	1981	761	1712	372	2415	744	1724
Environmental													
Labor Hours	Regular	398	413	400	400	440	480	440	440	424	466	432	432
	Overtime	34	51	0	0	58	87	144	216	53	80	102	153
Labor Cost	Regular	6221	6422	6232	6268	6904	7546	6882	6899	6678	7353	6834	6860
	Overtime	795	1186	0	0	1364	2050	3371	5070	1257	1889	2425	3651

again as John left. Not more than a few seconds later he poked his head back in the door. Cautiously eying the pencil in Lina's hand, he said, "Oh yeah, I forgot. You better include a couple different scenarios about the number of locations we'll have, if that makes any difference." He ducked out before Lina had time to throw something at him.

The next day John arranged to talk with Chuck Meyers and Dave Fast. Chuck was the Senior Vice President of Marketing. Dave was the Sales Manager. Because he thought that some of the information they would discuss would be of use to Lina, and because he thought she would benefit generally from being in on discussions such as this, he invited her to participate in the meeting.

Lina prepared a summary of the points made by each of the people and, after lunch, put the following notes on John's desk.

NOTES FROM CHUCK MEYERS

The industrial hygiene market is growing at about 6–8% per year. It will probably continue to do so for the next 10 years. The environmental market is projected to grow at an annual rate of 30% for the next five years and then begin to level out a bit after that. The asbestos (microscopy) market will stay at the same level, maybe grow 2–3% per year for the next three or four years and then begin dropping by as much as 10–15% per year thereafter. We should be able to increase our market share—that's why I hired Dave and the other three salesmen. If we market aggressively, and if we sell aggressively, we ought to be able to double our sales every year for the next three years. This whole business is populated with little mom-and-pop type labs started by chemists who had a couple pieces of equipment. Only three or four other labs have any real "business" sense—they're all run by scientists, technicians with no sense of marketing.

One thing that helps us is our turnaround time. We're generally more ready to offer "rush" service. Most labs offer standard 10-day turnaround. We offer 7-day turnaround on most analyses. And probably 20–25% of our work comes in on a rush basis. We offer 3-day, 48-hour, and, in some cases, 24-hour rush service. These really help the revenue picture because we charge 25%, 50%, and 100% premiums for the rush jobs.

The customized form of our report really helps with some customers, especially the new ones. Most labs simply send the customer a printout with the numbers, the chemical concentrations, on it. This is okay for those customers who have their own industrial hygienist or environmental officer who understands those numbers. But, for those customers who don't have that kind of expertise in house, our "plain English" report makes it a lot easier for them to understand the results of the analysis. We not only include the analytic results, we include the federal and state tolerance limits for the chemicals found, and we plainly state the results and possible consequences of the concentration levels in their samples.

The biggest problem is getting the jobs out on time. If there is one thing that's important, other than accuracy, of course, it's getting the customer the results when they are promised.

NOTES FROM DAVE FAST

Competition on prices is getting tougher and tougher. We've had to drop the prices on many of our analyses by 30% or more in the last two years. Still, lots of times we have to discount our published prices. On some items we're priced higher than the other guys, but we get the sale because we have a reputation for good quality.

Even those companies with industrial hygienists or environmental officers like the "plain English" form of our report. Since they often have to include the analytic results in their own report to their management or to a government agency, we save them a lot of work. A lot of them just attach our report to a cover letter and send it off that way. True, it is a lot of extra work producing the report this way. It seems that things get delayed over in "reports" a lot. I wish they could get their act together a little better.

We do sometimes sell something that isn't on the catalog list. We have to do that to keep certain customers happy. My salesmen don't want to have the customer go to another lab. They might stay with the other lab. Most of the time the salesman checks with the lab before selling one of the "special" orders. They are supposed to check all the time, but lots of times they just don't have time, or they can't get hold of the lab supervisor, or they just forget. It's usually not anything terribly exotic. It shouldn't be any big deal.

We'll get the orders into the lab; it's up to you guys in the labs to get them back out.

Later that afternoon, John got together with the laboratory managers and the supervisor of the microscopy laboratory. The discussion with Ron, Dennis, and Patricia went on for more than two hours. He took brief notes of the main points that each of the three made during the meeting.

Ron	It'll be really hard to hire and train people fast enough to keep up with that kind of growth. Doubt that she can pull it off.
Patricia	Asbestos business is going to drop off in a few years.
Ron	Most of growth will have to be in environmental, we're not very good at routine analyses right now.
	SRL built its reputation for high quality in IH and Microscopy; Environmental needs to catch up.
	We can get stuff out and we're getting better.
	Only been here a month and already identified a number of things that need fixing.
	Need to retrain everybody in the lab.
	They've gotten away from following the prescribed methodologies to the letter; must be followed exactly or results could be unreliable.
Dennis	IH chemists follow the analytic protocols; Marta and Jim make sure of that.
	If we get much bigger here, my supervisors will be overloaded.
Ron	Bad results leave us open to a lawsuit.
	Our equipment is outdated.
Dennis	Equipment in IH is pretty bad too.
	GCs (gas chromatographs) are old.
	They still give accurate results but it's getting slower and harder to ensure that accuracy.
	We need new detectors for all of the GCs.
	The GCs in all our labs are at least one generation out of date.
	The precision in the results seems less than it used to be.
Ron	There is equipment that we need but don't have.
Dennis	Newest technology in IH inorganics uses lasers to vaporize the samples, then analyzes light spectrum of resultant gas to identify the metals.
	Can do more, maybe five times the analyses per hour.

Patricia	Most of these things apply to the Microscopy lab, but maybe not as dramatically.
	Equipment is old and somewhat out of date.
	Without investing large amounts of money, couldn't make enough improvement to justify the cost.
Ron	We could improve productivity and quality if we had better equipment.
Dennis	If we had autosamplers on all GCs, chemist could easily do twice as many analyses.
Patricia	We need to buy electron microscopes so we can do other types of microscopy, or we'll have to get out of the microscopy business.
Ron	But we can't generate enough profit to pay off our debt and buy the new equipment without the improved productivity.
	Newest data systems allow analytic results to be sent electronically to report writing, eliminates chemists writing down results, writing the analysis, shuffling paper.
	We would probably at least double our labor productivity if we got this system.
	There would be fewer errors in transcribing and preparing the reports.
	Less supervision time needed for proofreading reports.
	Can also tie into accounting for automatic billing, cost analysis, etc.
Dennis	We need a better purchasing and inventory system.
	Things are 100% better since hiring Sam Bishop.
	Bishop struggling with a totally inadequate system.
	If we grow as planned, purchasing and inventory will get completely out of hand.

Returning to his office, John put his notes from the meeting in his briefcase and headed for the car. On the drive home, he began to think about what had been said in both of today's meetings. "Many of the ideas we discussed had been brought up before. Some of them were strategic in nature, but many of them were operational and tactical. Perhaps ultimately the operational and tactical issues are strategic, especially in a competitive environment, and especially if we are going to grow rapidly. What I have to do now is turn these into a workable strategic plan."

COMPANY 6

TRANSDUCER TECHNOLOGY

CASE 1

Transducer Technology: Statistical Quality Control

Richard Shuhi, Manufacturing Engineering Manager for Transducer Technology, Inc. (TTI), sat looking at his notes from the management staff meeting that had taken place earlier in the morning. One of the items on the agenda had been a discussion of a problem with the yield rate on the 265T15 transducer. Historically the yield from the production of 265T15 has been at or above the target of 97%. He looked at the Scrap Ledger for the 265T15 that he had started keeping about two months ago (Table 1). He had set this table up using a spreadsheet program on his personal computer. Until just a few days ago there had never really been a problem with the sensitivity of the 265T15, but there certainly seemed to be a problem now. The rate of failure due to low sensitivity had increased from less than 0.5% to more than 5%, and no one has been able to figure out why.

TTI is located in a new industrial park on the southwest side of St. Croix in the U.S. Virgin Islands and is an assembly division of Endevco, Inc., a large design, manufacturing, and distribution company headquartered in California. Transducers are devices that convert energy from one form into another. The transducers made by TTI convert physical energy (such as motion or vibrations) into electrical impulses. The 265T15 is a small transducer measuring 0.150" wide by 0.180" long by 0.060" thick. The heart of the 265T15 is a crystal measuring 0.070" wide by 0.100" long by 0.020" thick. The crystal is enclosed in a two-piece ceramic carrier that is held together with conductive and structural epoxy. There are no electrical leads into or out of the casing; the conductive epoxy acts as the signal transmitter (see Figure 1). The 265T15 detects

TABLE 1 Scrap Ledger. Model 265T15; Std.Hrs/Unit 0.505; Scrap Factor 5%

Operator Stamp #	Lot #	Build Qty	Describe Defect						Lot Yield(%) Goal: 96%
			Hi Cap	Low Cap	Low Res	Low Sens	No Output	Other	
02/18/93	08143-1	50	0	1					98
	08143-2	50	0				2	1	94
	08143-4	50	0	2					96
	08143-5	50	2					1	94
02/22/93	08143-3	50	0					1	98
02/24/93	08143-6	50	0					1	98
	08143-7	50							100
02/25/93	08143-8	50	1						98
	08143-10	50							100
03/01/93	08143-9	50	1						98
	08143-12	50	1	1			2		92
03/03/93	08143-11	50	0	0				1	98
03/10/93	08143-13	50	0				1		98
	08143-14	50	0					1	98
03/24/93	08143-15	50	0						100
	08143-16	50	0						100
	08143-17	50							100
03/30/93	08143-19	50	0				1		98
	08143-18	50	1					1	96
03/31/93	08148-1	50							100
	08148-2	50							100
04/01/93	08148-3	50							100
	08148-4	50							100

(continued)

TABLE 1 (continued)

Operator Stamp #	Lot #	Build Qty	Describe Defect						Lot Yield(%) Goal: 96%
			Hi Cap	Low Cap	Low Res	Low Sens	No Output	Other	
04/06/93	08148-5	50	0					1	98
	08148-6	50							100
	08148-7	50	0	2		0	1	1	92
	08148-8	50							100
	08148-9	50	0				2	2	92
04/07/93	08148-10	50	0	1				2	94
	08146-9	50							100
04/15/93	08150-1	50	2	2				4	84
	08150-2	50	0					2	96
	08150-3	50	0				1	1	96
	08150-4	50							100
04/16/93	08150-5	50							100
04/19/93	08150-6	50	1					3	92
	08150-7	50	1	1				4	88
	08150-8	50							100
	08150-9	50							100
	08153-1	50	0					2	96
	08153-2	50	0					7	86
04/21/93	08153-3	50	0				0	17	66
	08153-4	50	0				3	8	78
04/22/93	08153-6	47	0						100
04/27/93	08153-5	50							100
04/28/93	08153-10	50							100

(continued)

TABLE 1 (continued)

Operator Stamp #	Lot #	Build Qty	Describe Defect						Lot Yield(%) Goal: 96%
			Hi Cap	Low Cap	Low Res	Low Sens	No Output	Other	
	08154-1	50	2						96
	08154-2	50							100
	08154-3	50							100
	08154-4	50	0					1	98
	08154-5	50							100
04/29/93	08154-6	50							100
	08154-7	50							100
05/03/93	08153-8	50	2			4	0	2	84
	08153-9	50				3		1	92
	08154-8	50							100
05/04/93	08153-11	50	0						96
	08156-3	50	0					2	96
	08153-12	50	2						100
	08153-7	50	0			1			96
05/05/93	08156-1	50	1					1	96
	08156-5	50	0						100
	08153-13	50	0						100
	08156-2	50							100
	08156-6	50							100
05/06/93	08156-4	50							100
05/11/93	08153-14	50							100
05/12/93	08156-7	50		1				1	98
	08154-9	50							98

(continued)

TABLE 1 (continued)

Operator Stamp #	Lot #	Build Qty	Describe Defect						Lot Yield(%) Goal: 96%
			Hi Cap	Low Cap	Low Res	Low Sens	No Output	Other	
	08156-9	50							100
	08154-10	50							100
	08156-10	50	1						98
	08157-4	50							100
05/13/93	08156-8	50							100
	08157-5	50		6					88
	08157-10	50	3					2	90
	08157-2	50						1	98
	08157-1	50	1					2	94
	08157-3	50						0	100
05/19/93	08159-1	50						1	98
	08159-5	50						1	98
	08159-4	50	1						98
	08157-8	50	3						94
	08159-2	50	1					1	96
05/20/93	08159-3	50						0	100
	08157-9	50				1	1		96
	08157-6	50	1						98
	08159-6	50						0	100
	08159-8	50	1						98
	08159-7	50						0	100
	08157-7	50	1			10	1		76
05/26/93	08161-4	50	2			2		1	90

(continued)

TABLE 1 (continued)

Operator Stamp #	Lot #	Build Qty	Describe Defect						Lot Yield(%) Goal: 96%
			Hi Cap	Low Cap	Low Res	Low Sens	No Output	Other	
	08159-9	50	2			1			94
	08161-1	50						0	100
	08159-10	50	3						94
	08161-3	50						0	100
	08161-8	50				3		1	92
	08161-2	50				2			96
	08161-5	50				3			94
05/27/93	08161-7	50				2		1	94
	08162-1	50				2			96
	08162-2	50				10		2	76
06/01/93	08161-6	50						2	96
06/03/93	08161-9	50				4			92
	08162-8	50			1				98
	08162-6	50	1						98
06/07/93	08162-5	50		1				17	64
	08162-3	50	2			11			74
	08162-4	50				3	1	1	90
06/08/93	08162-10	50						2	96
	08162-9	50						0	100
	08162-7	50				1			98
	08162-11	50	1					2	94
	08162-12	50						0	100
06/12/93	08164-6	50				1		1	96

(continued)

TABLE 1 (continued)

Operator Stamp #	Lot #	Build Qty	Describe Defect						Lot Yield(%) Goal: 96%
			Hi Cap	Low Cap	Low Res	Low Sens	No Output	Other	
	08162-14	50						0	100
	08162-15	50				9			82
	08164-2	50						0	100
06/14/93	08162-13	50				1			98
	08164-4	50	3						94
	08164-3	50	1			1		1	94
06/15/93	08164-1	50				1		1	98
	08164-5	50	1						98
06/17/93	08164-7	50				1			98
06/22/93	08165-4	50						0	100
	08165-3	50						4	92
	08164-8	50			1				98
	08164-9	50				4			92
06/23/93	08165-2	50	1						98
	08164-10	50				3			94
	08165-9	50					1		98
	08165-5	50	1						98
06/24/93	08165-1	50				3			94
	08165-7	50						0	100
	08165-10	50				2		2	92
	08165-8	50				1			98
	08165-1	50				1			98
Total		6847	48	19	2	90	17	115	95.75%

189

Figure 1   *265T15 Transducer (Exploded View)*

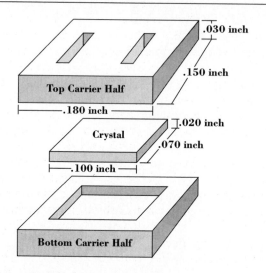

Note:

Conductive epoxy is applied to the top carrier half to fix the crystal. Sufficient epoxy must be applied to fill the contact slots in the top carrier half. Structural epoxy is applied to the bottom carrier half to bond the two halves together and seal the assembly.

small vibrations and emits electrical impulses based on the frequency and magnitude of the vibrations. Typically the 265T15 is sold to companies to be used in R&D studies of the effects of vibration on materials or products or it is designed into products as a part of a closed-loop control system. The transducer detects vibration and sends a small electrical impulse which may, in turn, initiate a response to the vibration. One of the biggest sources of demand for the 265T15 at the present is from a firm making heart pacemakers. When the pacemaker is implanted in a person, the 265T15 detects vibrations caused by the individual's pulse. The resulting signals from the 265T15 are interpreted by logic incorporated in a microchip in the pacemaker, which then sends stimuli to control the pace of the person's heart.

The actual production process is a relatively simple batch process, though it is delicate because of the small size of the product. In a clean and well-ventilated area, a worker visually inspects the individual crystals from a lot number kit under a microscope. If they appear sound, they are glued into the top half of the carrier using conductive epoxy. The top half of the carrier has two slots through which the epoxy provides electrical contact to the ends of the crystal. After the assembly has cured, about four hours, the bottom half of the carrier is glued in place using structural (nonconductive) epoxy. The entire assembly is then heat cured, cleaned, and polished. Final measurements and physical inspections are performed on each chip prior to release. All of the assembly takes place under microscopes using very small, high-precision tools and fixtures. Considerable manual labor and very little automation are involved in the process. Generally one worker processes a complete batch. Because of the idle time while the epoxy is curing, a worker typically has several batches in process at any given moment.

Up until a few weeks ago, TTI had been producing an average of 600 265T15s per week. That output has dropped to about 500 per week. The decline is due strictly to a decline in demand. The decline in demand is due to slower business being experienced by TTI's customers due, almost entirely, to general economic conditions. None of the drop in demand is due to production quality problems. Richard was quite sure that very, very few, if any, bad units were ever shipped to a customer. The assemblers on the production floor personally inspect and test every unit produced. Any units not passing inspection are put aside for the quality engineer to test and inspect. The purpose of the quality engineer's testing and inspection is to verify the unit's failure and to classify the reason for failure. If the quality engineer cannot identify the cause of the failure, a manufacturing engineer will be brought in to help with the analysis.

The assemblers' 100% inspection is only part of the quality control at TTI. Typically a customer sends an engineering and quality inspection team to TTI to do a quality audit of the production and quality systems. Only after TTI passes the customer audit is a contract negotiated. In the case of the 265T15, TTI had passed the customer audit with flying colors. TTI has extensive documentation for describing the assembly process and procedures, including standards and procedures for the inspection and testing of every unit assembled. On a regular basis, manufacturing engineering and quality engineering do internal audits to verify that the assembly and quality procedures are being followed properly. If the audit turns up problems that the assemblers have not been detecting, an investigation is undertaken to discover the reason for the problem (and the reason why it was not detected) and corrective actions are initiated. The final step in the quality process is to include certain parts of the documentation with the product as it is delivered to the customer. The documentation sent to the customer includes:

- A copy of all the test data for each lot, which includes a listing of all failures and data for a random sample of 4% of the acceptable transducers.

- A lot control sheet for each lot, which certifies each step in the production process was properly performed (Figure 2).
- The audit worksheet for each lot, which includes cosmetic as well as functional evaluation of a sample of ten units from each lot.

The assemblers' inspection and the quality engineering audit focus on five specifications, three electrical and two physical. The three electrical specifications are sensitivity of the transducer to picking up vi-

Figure 2   Lot Control Sheet

Transducer Technology
Lot Control Traveler

Initial [ ]

Work Order # _____   Date _____

Lot #s _____   Piece Part ID #s

_____   _____

_____   _____

_____   _____

Record all information concerning the Work Order and all component parts.

1	2	3	4	5	6
7	8	9	10	11	12
13	14	15	16	17	18

Operation # Check Block
Stamp each block as the corresponding process operation number is completed.

Comments _____

_____

_____

_____

_____

Record all non-conformities, problems, failures, or other relevent events for this Work Order.

brations, capacitance, and resistance. The two physical specifications are dimensions (the size of the finished unit) and visual appearance. For every internal audit, a worksheet is prepared summarizing the data (Figure 3). If the average value of the sample falls within the specification limits, the audit worksheet is filed for possible future review. If the audit detects any problems, investigative action is started to find and eliminate the cause of the problem. Table 2 summarizes the last fifteen internal audits.

Figure 3   *265T15 Audit Worksheet*

Record Sensitivity, Resistance, and Capacitance readings

Applicable Specs: IM: 32-024-501 Rev.8.1 Endco 265T15 and 265T15A

Reading #	Sensitivity 1.5-2.5 pc/g	Capacitance 440-660 pF	Resistance 100 GΩ Min	Dimensional Refer to 129-0001-3101:	Visual
1	1.82	546	✓	✓	✓
2	1.90	543	✓	✓	✓
3	1.85	539	✓	✓	✓
4	1.79	552	✓	✓	✓
5	1.84	537	✓	✓	✓
6	1.86	543	✓	✓	✓
7	1.96	545	✓	✓	✓
8	1.82	549	✓	✓	✓
9	1.77	543	✓	✓	✓
10	1.93	548	✓	✓	✓
Average	1.85	544.5			
Range	.19	15.0			
Date:	5/04/93	5/06/93	5/06/93	5/06/93	5/06/93
By:	Robert Vifo	Robert Vifo	Robert Vifo	Robert Vifo	Robert Vifo
P/N:	22M5A	22M5A	22M5A	22M5A	22M5A
Lot #	08153-12	08156-6	08156-6	08156-2	08156-5

Note: These audit sheets must be completed daily and on a random basis. Each of the audit elements (sensitivity, capacitance, resistance, dimensional, and visual) should not be done on the same day each week.

TABLE 2   TTI 265T15 Audit Results Feb.–June, 1993

Sensitivity Values - 1.5-2.5 pC/g Standard

Sample	1	2	3	4	5	6	7
Lot #	08143-5	08143-10	08143-11	08143-17	08148-4	08148-8	08150-6
Date	02/17/93	02/24/93	03/02/93	03/24/93	04/01/93	04/06/93	04/14/93
Reading							
1	1.92	1.85	1.95	1.81	1.88	1.80	1.82
2	1.91	1.95	2.00	1.90	1.79	1.83	1.84
3	1.93	1.93	1.86	1.89	1.86	2.00	2.00
4	1.89	1.90	1.94	1.94	2.00	1.89	1.90
5	1.81	1.91	1.84	1.88	1.91	1.83	1.85
6	1.86	1.90	1.87	1.92	1.97	1.73	1.77
7	1.79	1.83	1.88	1.82	1.86	1.90	1.94
8	1.96	1.89	1.87	1.87	1.93	1.89	1.90
9	1.76	1.88	1.85	1.92	1.95	1.84	1.83
10	1.94	1.70	1.85	1.89	1.83	1.82	1.82

Capacitance Values - 440-660 pF Standard

Sample	1	2	3	4	5	6	7
Lot #	08143-3	08143-6	08143-13	08143-15	08143-19	08146-9	08150-2
Date	02/17/93	02/23/93	03/09/93	03/23/93	03/24/93	04/07/93	04/14/93
Reading							
1	625	583	607	574	577	588	565
2	536	581	576	587	578	619	532
3	534	614	579	571	586	547	536
4	538	581	555	543	578	582	564
5	527	555	586	592	578	585	558
6	543	558	574	581	582	603	568
7	545	515	585	565	568	589	566
8	549	619	554	571	564	583	553
9	537	573	577	592	560	590	538
10	531	555	534	538	579	594	575

Assembly of the 265T15 product started about five months ago. Initially the units tested were quite stable and within tolerances for the three electrical specifications. Some problems with yield in lots 08150-1, 08150-7, and 08153-1 through 08153-4 were traced to assemblers not correctly following the assembly procedures. These problems were

TABLE 2   (continued)

8 08153-3 04/20/93	9 08154-5 04/27/93	10 08153-12 05/04/93	11 08154-10 05/12/93	12 08157-7 05/18/93	13 08161-2 05/26/93	14 08162-5 06/03/93	15 08162-11 06/07/93
1.76	1.86	1.82	1.90	1.96	1.64	1.61	1.88
1.91	1.90	1.90	1.86	1.50	1.61	1.66	1.83
1.74	1.78	1.85	1.75	1.50	1.63	1.63	1.80
1.76	1.83	1.79	1.91	1.71	1.72	1.50	1.87
1.80	1.87	1.84	1.81	1.53	1.65	1.55	1.77
1.78	1.81	1.86	1.70	1.76	1.67	1.52	1.76
1.73	1.86	1.96	1.95	1.49	1.68	1.51	1.82
1.85	1.84	1.82	1.83	1.71	1.86	1.62	1.83
1.82	1.80	1.77	1.90	1.45	1.65	1.45	1.81
1.78	1.85	1.93	1.76	1.84	1.60	1.64	1.96

8 08153-4 04/21/93	9 08154-3 04/26/93	10 08156-6 05/06/93	11 08153-14 05/10/93	12 08159-1 05/18/93	13 08161-3 05/25/93	14 08162-5 06/03/93	15 08162-12 06/08/93
570	549	546	560	511	562	539	557
574	570	543	562	516	501	510	561
583	573	539	552	535	551	547	548
579	582	552	567	521	541	526	545
586	569	537	580	515	563	508	524
547	562	543	569	521	536	518	522
575	551	545	543	528	552	524	539
571	584	549	542	537	555	533	531
589	579	543	516	551	567	523	543
590	581	548	558	532	539	514	527

corrected and, with the exception of a brief relapse of the same noncon-
formance problem during lots 08153-8 and 08153-9, the yield has been acceptable. An unusual problem occurred on lot 08162-2. One of the
assemblers accidentally knocked a tray of crystals off the assembly bench
and they fell to the tile floor. The crystals are quite fragile and the

impact caused many to develop hairline fractures and small chips, most of which the assemblers detected during the assembly process. But the damage made them unusable for the 265T15 product.

During the first week in June, the assemblers voiced some concerns to the manufacturing engineer. The assemblers felt that the sensitivity of the units did not appear to be as high as it had been in the past. The average sensitivity is still well within the tolerance limits, but the mean value of the sensitivity seemed to have decreased and more units seemed to be failing because of inadequate sensitivity.

The specifications for sensitivity call for a target value of 2.000 pC/g, with upper and lower specification limits of 1.500 pC/g and 2.500 pC/g. During February and March the sensitivity had been hovering around 1.890 pC/g. Although this is below the target of 2.000 pC/g, it was well within acceptable limits. Since mid May, however, the average has been considerably lower. This is particularly significant because customers view low sensitivity as a very bad condition. On the other hand, customers view high sensitivity very favorably, as long as it is within the specification limit.

The shift in the process mean seems to have contributed to a lower yield rate. Although it does not affect TTI's reputation in the marketplace (since all the bad units are caught before they leave the plant), it does hurt economically. The cost for materials and labor in a 265T15 is about $37.12. Any unit failing inspection is scrapped because it is impossible to rework.

Both manufacturing engineering and quality engineering have started to take a much closer look at the assembly process. Although sensitivity is the most important performance dimension of the 265T15 product, capacitance is also tested and recorded. The actual value of the capacitance is not very critical. The upper and lower specification limits are 440 pF and 660 pF, respectively. This is quite a broad range. TTI tries to hit the midpoint, but variations within specification are not considered very important. The measure of capacitance does serve a useful purpose. Changes in capacitance generally indicate a variation in some other aspect of the product—a variation that is not directly measurable. A casual examination of the capacitance tests by manufacturing engineering has suggested that such a change might be occurring.

The entire St. Croix engineering staff has talked with the design engineer in California to discuss possible causes of the problem. They have identified crystals, the assembly processes, and the environment as the most likely sources of the problem. The crystals are manufactured by a subcontractor in Texas and shipped to the main facility in San Juan Capistrano, California. The ceramic carriers are manufactured by a company in Colorado and also shipped to California. The Capistrano plant does basic acceptance sampling on the crystals and carriers, but no real detailed inspection. The crystals and carriers are repackaged as a kit, given a lot number designation, and shipped from California to St. Croix for assembly. The kits are shipped in lot number order, but they are not necessarily assembled in that order in St. Croix.

The quality engineers and the manufacturing engineers in the St. Croix facility have discussed the problem with the assemblers. Inspection of work-in-process has been increased to look for variances. However, all the assembly processes are being done exactly as prescribed in the documentation. Richard does not believe that the environment in the St. Croix plant has changed in any significant fashion during the last several months. In short, the cause for the decreased sensitivity is a mystery. Richard put down his notes from the management staff meeting, sat back in his chair, and stared up at the ceiling. "I have no idea what is happening here. The yields are going down. I seem to have some quality problems, yet the processes and the materials seem to check out just fine. Maybe I need to go through this whole analysis process again with a fresh outlook to see if there is anything I have missed. Sometimes we can be too close to the problem to see it!"

CASE 2

Transducer Technology: Aggregate Planning, Capacity, and Inventory

Transducer Technology, Inc. (TTI), located on the island of St. Croix in the U.S. Virgin Islands, produces a variety of transducers. Transducers are devices that convert energy from one form into another. The transducers made by TTI convert physical energy (such as motion or vibrations) into electrical impulses. TTI is owned by Endevco, Inc., which is located in San Juan Capistrano, California. Endevco has centralized several of the planning functions, of which forecasting is one. Thus TTI does no forecasting of its own. TTI simply plans to be able to build and ship the quantities that Endevco orders. TTI builds both to stock and to order. Each month TTI receives a shipment plan from Endevco. The shipment plan has a rolling four-month horizon. Each month's plan contains the required shipments for the coming month plus a forecast of what the shipments will be for the following three months.

The shipment requirements for the coming month are treated as firm. Changes are not made to the shipment quantities unless absolutely necessary. The forecasts for the subsequent months are not firm. The forecast for the second month out is generally pretty close to what the final numbers will look like. There are, inevitably, some changes. The third and fourth months are subject to considerable change, usually increases in the demand requirements.

Over the last eighteen months, TTI has been moving toward semi-autonomous work teams on the production floor. Three supervisors provide leadership, coaching, training, and other assistance to the twelve production teams. Each team builds a number of different products or subassemblies. The different products or subassemblies built by any one team are, for the most part, all similar in design, complexity, and assembly procedures. Once the shipment plan is received, the production team, with help from its supervisor, develops a production schedule and informs the materials management department of the team's materials needs for the next four months.

Paul Smith is the supervisor for the Best-in-the-West team. (The team name refers to the fact that TTI is located in the western part of the island.) The Best-in-the-West team builds thirteen different final products. For purposes of developing the weekly build schedule, the team schedules each of the thirteen items separately. If the monthly demand requires fewer labor-hours than the team has available, the team plans to produce the quantities that Endevco requested. If, however, the quantities Endevco requested require more labor-hours than are available in any month, the team then develops a monthly aggregate production plan to cover the entire four-month planning horizon. Their decision criteria is to develop a plan that will minimize the labor cost. For purposes of this aggregate planning, the thirteen individual products are grouped into three categories. Within each category the products are very similar in terms of the resources (especially labor) that they consume. These three groups are treated as three pseudo-products, and the monthly aggregate production plan is developed for these three pseudo-products.

When the shipment plan for May-to-August was received in early April 1993, it was evident that demand for May exceeded labor availability. Consequently Paul and the Best-in-the-West team set about the task of developing an aggregate plan for the next four months. Endevco's shipment plan demand is shown in Table 1.

The standard labor-hours for the three pseudo-products are:

Group	Labor-Hours/Unit
A	2.5
B	2.8
C	3.2

These labor standards are "yielded" standards. That is, they include allowances for the normal process yield so no adjustments are necessary to allow for scrap. For example, if 100 units are required and the yield is 97%, it will probably be necessary to make 103 or 104 units to get 100 acceptable units. Since the yield is already considered in the labor standard, the estimated labor-hours required will be 100 units multiplied by

TABLE 1   Shipment Plan - May/Aug, 1993

	Item	May	June	July	Aug
Group A	2221D				8
	2221F	30		35	25
	Total	30	0	35	33
Group B	2223D	4	20		10
	2224C				
	224C-	125	110	100	50
	2225			25	
	2225M5A	20			
	Total	149	130	125	60
Group C	2226C	126	15	85	75
	2228C		45	20	20
	2258-10	21	12	12	
	2258-100	13			
	30708-2	85		30	30
	7221	35			25
	Total	280	72	147	150

the unit standard time. This significantly simplifies the labor estimation process. Further, by incorporating the yield into the labor standard, it cannot be inadvertently forgotten during the estimation process.

The Best-in-the-West team has five members who each work 40 hours per week. For planning purposes, overtime is limited to 20% of regular time. The average wage rate is currently $7.80 per hour, but that is scheduled to increase by 8% (to $8.42) on July 1, 1993. Overtime is paid at time-and-a-half. TTI uses a 4, 4, 5 budget cycle for fixing the number of weeks in a month. Thus May has four weeks, June has five weeks, and July and August each have four weeks.

Sometimes it is necessary (or desirable) to produce units before they are needed. When they do, a monthly inventory carrying cost estimated at 5% of the labor cost of a unit is charged against the production budget. For example, if a unit contains $50 worth of labor, the inventory carrying cost is $2.50 per month. Further, if TTI delivers orders late, a late delivery penalty is charged to the production budget. This charge covers the costs of backordering, lost sales, and loss of customer good will. The current late delivery penalty charges are as follows:

Late Delivery Time	Group		
	A	B	C
One month late	$11.23	$12.48	$14.26
Two months late	$19.27	$21.41	$24.47

The Best-in-the-West team has gotten really excited about the production planning process, but they realize their current approach is less than perfect. It is a heuristic process that attempts to level the workload over the four-month planning horizon. Although the schedules are always feasible, the team feels they could develop a lower cost solution with a more sophisticated model. One of the team members came across some information about linear optimization models, and the team is interested in knowing more. They have asked Paul for some information about building a model that will optimize the aggregate production plan. "Usually these type of ideas come from the staff people in a company," Paul thought as the team meeting broke up. "But these guys are really motivated. It's no problem getting some basic linear programming information, but I better get to work on this right now. I'd hate to have their enthusiasm cool because of my inactivity."

CASE 3 Transducer Technology: Process Design, Line Balancing, and Layout

Richard Shuhi, Manufacturing Engineering Manager for Transducer Technology, Inc., sat down at his desk and put the notes from the A-Team meeting in a new folder. "This," he thought, "is going to require some careful analysis." One of the main items for discussion had been problems the A-Team is having building the four products for which it is responsible. The A-Team is one of TTI's twelve semi-autonomous production teams. It has four products that it builds on a regular basis (Table 1).

The three models bearing numbers beginning with the letter "T" are transducers, devices that convert energy from one form into another. These transducers convert physical energy (such as motion, physical shock, or vibrations) into electrical impulses. The C420-A is a cable that connects to various transducers, including the three built by the A-Team. The T422-1 and T424-C are small, lightweight uniaxial transduc-

TABLE 1 A-Team Production

Model	Build Time (Std Hrs/Unit)	Quantity (per Month)
T422-1	1.9	75
T422-3	5.5	40
T424-C	1.7	200
C420-A	0.8	250

ers. They detect changes in motion along a single axis. They measure about 0.125" wide by 0.250" long by 0.125" thick. The T422-3 is also small and lightweight, but it is triaxial. It detects motion along three perpendicular axes. It is cubical, measuring about 0.375" on each side. One of the principal applications for the T422-3 is in the crash testing of automobiles. Several transducers are attached to or built into the crash-test dummies to detect the direction and magnitude of shocks to various parts of the body in auto crashes. Another frequent application is in testing the shock-proofing performance of packaging of electronic instruments.

At the present time the five members of the A-Team work independently. Parts for a lot of 25 units are kitted and given to a team member to assemble from start to finish. Sometimes two or more team members work together on a lot, but even then they still each build their own units from start to finish. The layout of the shop floor in the transducer assembly area is shown in Figure 1.

Deciding whether to build a lot individually or collectively is left up to the team members. Records are kept to allow tracking of individual units back to the employee who built it, so working collectively poses no problems with traceability. The team members generally enjoy working collectively. It makes it easier for them to discuss problems with the work and to help each other. It also gives them a little more common ex-

Figure 1   *Shop Floor Layout Transducer Assembly Area*

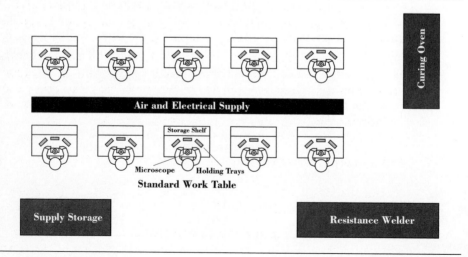

perience to share with one another. This social aspect seems important
to them.

Each team member works 40 hours per week. TTI divides each 13-
week quarter into two months with four weeks, followed by a month
with five weeks. TTI's months correspond roughly, but not exactly, to
the calendar months. With five members on the team, this provides a
base of 800 labor-hours for a four-week month and 1000 labor-hours for
a five-week month. These numbers are reduced by holidays (17 per
year), vacations (2.4 weeks per person per year on average), and per-
sonal/sick days (5.3 per person per year on average).

The quantity numbers cited in Table 1 are averages, but there is an
effort to keep them pretty steady so that the production schedule will be
as linear as possible. One of the main problems discussed in the meeting
this morning was the amount of overtime being worked by the A-Team.
Richard had investigated the time standards and concluded that they
are pretty accurate, with one exception. There seems to be more delay
occurring than has been built into the standards.

TTI has built a 10% P, R & D (personal, rest, and delay) factor into
all their production standards, but the A-Team is experiencing more
than this. One of the primary reasons for the delay is that two of the
process operations for the 422s and one operation for the 424s require
the use of a resistance welder. This is an expensive piece of equipment
and TTI has only one. Although the welder setup is virtually the same
for all models (less than five minutes is required for a change over),
more than one assembler frequently needs to use the welder at the same
time. When this happens, one of the assemblers has to wait. Sometimes
he or she may be able to do something productive during the delay, but
often they cannot. They are each working on only one lot at a time.
When the process gets to the point of needing the resistance welder, it
needs the welder. The cost of the welder, and the relatively small frac-
tion of time it is in use, make it impractical to buy a second unit. At the
meeting it was decided that Richard would investigate the ramifications
of redesigning the assembly process of the transducers built by the A-
Team. The proposed change would involve moving away from the current individual batch system to a multistation flow line.

The assembly for all three transducer units involves three stages:

1. Assembly of the seismic subassembly
2. Assembly of the case subassembly
3. Final assembly of the case and the seismic subassemblies into the
   final transducer unit.

The current process documentation for the T422-1 Transducer is
shown in Table 2. Stages 1 and 2 can be done independently of one an-

TABLE 2 Process Documentation. Item T422-1. Effective Date: November 12, 1990

Operation Number		Description	Standard Time/Unit
	1	Unpack crystal, mask, and carrier lot record lot # on checksheet	0.044
	2	Arrange masks and crystal in holders	0.03344
Stage (1)	3	Place mask in position under microscope	0.099
	4	Position crystal over mask and inspect crystal	0.11
	5	Press crystal into place on mask	0.088
	6	Place assembly in holding rack	0.077

(Operations 3–6 will be repeated until the entire lot is processed.)

	7	Remove required amount of epoxy from freezer and load in dispenser	0.033
Stage (2)	8	Position top carrier half under microscope and inspect	0.099
	9	Apply epoxy in cable connector hole	0.11
	10	Insert cable connector	0.077
	11	Remove excess epoxy from assembly	0.11
	12	Place assembly in curing rack	0.099

(Operations 8–12 will be repeated until the entire lot is processed.)

	13	Place curing rack in oven to cure epoxy (temperature and time per daily operation chart)	0.0396
	14	Weld cable to cable connector using resistance welder	0.1925
Stage (3)	15	Position bottom carrier half under microscope and inspect	0.1375
	16	Insert connector bolt in bottom carrier half	0.11
	17	Align mask and crystal assembly in bottom carrier half and inspect	0.22
	18	Align top carrier half over bottom carrier assembly and affix locking nut to bolt Inspect entire assembly (Torque 10 cent./kilo)	0.22

(Operations 14–18 will be repeated until the entire lot is processed.)

Allowance Factor 10% included		Total Standard Time	1.9 hrs

Notes: Operations 1, 2, 7, and 13 are actually done once per batch.
Operation 13 consists of three separate activities: Transport curing rack to oven—0.09 hrs.; adjust, stabilize, and load oven—0.45 hrs.; and unload oven and inspect case assemblies—0.45 hrs. This does not include the oven cure time which averages 0.5 hours.

TABLE 3   Standard Times

	T422-1	T422-3	T424-C
Stage 1	0.7	0.7 (x3)	0.7
Stage 2	0.4	1.0	0.4
Stage 3	0.8	2.1	0.6
Total	1.9	5.2	1.7

other and/or in parallel. The tooling required for all three stages is identical for all the models. It is in the final assembly (stage 3) that the resistance welder is used (twice for each 422 unit and once for each 424 unit). The uniaxial 422-1 and 424 models each have a single seismic unit built into them. The 422-3 unit is triaxial and has three seismic subassemblies. The standard times for each of the stages are shown in Table 3.

Richard began to think about some alternatives he might investigate. "The assembly operations for all three units are so similar that we could mix the various models in the assembly flow. But that's a pretty sophisticated solution if all we're trying to do is remove a bottleneck at the welder. Still, it's worth looking at. But I'll bet moving the entire operation away from the batch process to a flow line would be simpler and it might accomplish our goal." He reached for a clean pad of paper and began to make some notes.